Peace & Love

THE TIME IS ALWAYS NOW

Leland Bedford

iUniverse LLC
Bloomington

PEACE & LOVE
THE TIME IS ALWAYS NOW

iUniverse books may be ordered through booksellers or by contacting:

iUniverse LLC
1663 Liberty Drive
Bloomington, IN 47403
www.iuniverse.com
1-800-Authors (1-800-288-4677)

ISBN: 978-1-4917-2387-6 (sc)
ISBN: 978-1-4917-2388-3 (e)

Printed in the United States of America.

iUniverse rev. date: 02/05/2014

Contents

Dedication

I dedicate this compilation of religious, spiritual, inspirational, and philosophical contemplations on life, death, Heaven, Hell, God, the Devil, math, science, you, me, and our purpose as human beings to all people that have life. The purpose of this book is to share my thoughts with all whom are willing to open their heart, mind, and soul, and collectively journey with me as I present a case for the greatest victory of all victories, *Peace & Love*. Through the journey I hope that all whom are willing find joy and happiness through what is discovered, and are inspired to explore the ideas that are presented while enjoying what is meant to spark the brain, warm the heart, renew the spirit, and manifest peace and love in all that you would do after our journey has ended. The idea of peace and love is what motivated this compilation and I accredit the completion to all that I have known, and will ever know in my lifetime. My life experiences, and life relationships, are reflected with in the pages of this book, whether good or bad, my influences are with in the ideas that appear on the pages of this book. My personal view on life and my understanding of death has lead me to appreciate peace and seek love, those things I believe are the only possibility to sustain all that we know as human beings that being life. In my life I have learned that problems are inevitable but solutions are not, this is a simple lesson I have learned to be true, and which has helped in my own personal development; through this understanding I feel that my purpose is not to solve all my problems, which may not be in as serious degree to others, but rather to find happiness with in myself, appreciate the peace that I have in my life, and seek love from them whom also are in search of it, together we will both have peace, and will have found love. In the end the meaning of this book is to provoke thought, and inspire truth, and crown peace and love as king, this I know has no flaw, and will never lead us astray. I dedicate this book to all whom find joy in the joyful, hope in faith, triumph from tragedy, truth in truth, peace in love, love in peace; and whom are willing to journey with me through the pages of this book, on a purposeful journey of thought, religion, spirituality, philosophy, inspiration, math and science, leading us to truth that *Peace & Love* is the way.

Acknowledgment

I would like to thank all that contributed to the completion of *Peace &*
Love. This book is a result of every experience, relationship, life lesson,
success and failure I have had in my lifetime, and I thank all that I
have known, naming no names to protect the innocent. Thank you for
making me a better man with all glory being to God. I would also like
to thank each person whom helped in bringing this book to the people,
I am forever grateful, if only one person were to read this book I feel
my purpose will have been served. In closing I would like to thank my
family whom I love, and whom has always been my main source for
inspiration and the backbone that has sustained me through life.

Preface

"Peace and Love" is a compilation of all original thoughts and ideas. All that is written is a product of my own personal thoughts, ideas, and philosophies. The book began as a result of a life time of contemplations which never manifested into tangible existence, but through the grace of God my thoughts found a home on the paper. The book consists of a large spectrum of material, from thought provoking quotes, philosophical contemplations, poetic prose, and inspirational words, all with the purpose of inspiring truth, love, victory, joy, and bring peace and love to all whom read it. The book it self is centered around the purpose of purpose, the hope of hope, the truth in life, and the lie in death, the answer of peace, and the reward of love. With peace and love being the center I believe that we can never be lead astray, and that all that journey with me will find the journey to be that which leads them to the center. Each selection from this book contributes to the whole but they are all vastly unique and will hopefully provoke thought, lighting a spark in the brain of all whom may read, to explore their own views on all that is explored. The completion of this book came as a result of my own personal understanding that the compilation was complete, but the book itself is something that can never truly be complete being that it is my thoughts on all we know to be true that being life, such contemplations can never truly be complete, they will eternally span the length of a lifetime. *Peace & Love* however reflects a certain period of my life, representing the whole of my existence, but being compiled with in a blessed place in time. In the end I hope that all whom are witness to this book, and whom journey through its pages, find peace and love, and are inspired to seek it in all that they may do.

Introduction

Peace & Love is collection of religious, spiritual, inspirational, and philosophical short passages, quotes, and poetry. The subject matter ranges from the idea of peace and love, good and evil, right and wrong, love and hate, truth and lie, you and me. The selections are all my original thoughts, ideas, and quotes and follow a logical ideological order as to guide you as the reader through my contemplative journey through truth leading to peace and love. The book reflects ideas centered around metaphysical thought, science vs. religion, truth vs. lie, mathematical relativity, inspirational words, with hope to inspire, honorable philosophies, and simply thoughts on peace and love. The hope of this book is to inspire all that may read to see balance in thought, and to add to their own personal knowledge and beliefs, and hopefully improve what was in need of improvement as man, woman, or child, as a human being. *Peace & Love* touches on serious subject matter which can be considered controversial by them whom are conservative in their beliefs, but its purpose is not to speak blasphemous against any religious denomination, or sect, but rather to explore truth and present ideas that invoke thought, by them whom respect truth, and seek understanding. Though much of the subject matter can be deemed serious, the underlined purpose in completing this book is to bring happiness and joy to all whom journey through its pages, with new knowledge and faith an inevitable fate. To all whom cross paths with this book I implore that regardless of any beliefs that my be held that you explore all that is with in its pages, with a open mind, and a open heart, and to be prepared to laugh, smile, and cry, because in the end the only result can be peace and love.

I.

The definition of peace is love, and the definition of love is peace. Together we define each other alone we have no meaning . . .

———————————— •❖• ————————————

The idea of peace is what I love. The idea that we can live together as one yet still be so different, with no hate between us, is peace. The idea of love is what I love. The possibility that someone can care for you as they care for them self is truly a blessing. It is the idea of hate that I hate. For someone to hate you is the equivalent to murder a justice that should only be delivered by our Father God. It is the idea of life that gives me purpose. To have life is to have hope, to have hope is to have faith, to have faith is to have God, to have God is to have everything.

———————————— •❖• ————————————

Peace can bring you hope, joy, happiness, prosperity, virtue, truth, wealth, wisdom, knowledge, love, resurrection, victory and defeat, life after death. What is peace is the question, the answer is serious. Love can overwhelm you, engulf you, smother you, protect you, surpass you, comfort you, manifest hatred, peace and war, guide you, heal you, drown you, define you. What is love is the question, the answer is what you need. Peace and love can bring family blessings, life long friendships, spiritual, mental, and physical health, tranquil tranquility, courage in the midst of war, patience that can span the test of time, a kings respect and power, prosperity in the midst of tragedy, new beginnings that will never end, guidance and leadership, truth. The question is what is peace and love, the answer is you.

Hate can never defeat love. Love is victory and has no ending, while hate is defeat and has no beginning. Love is beauty and has no flaw, while hate is pain and has no joy. Love builds, while hate destroys. Love is everlasting, while hate consumes like a cancer, never to be known, only to be forgotten. Love is purpose, while hate is its purpose. Love guides us through life, while hate leads us astray. We live by our love, while we die by our hate. With no love there is no life, while hate is death itself. Hate can never defeat love.

The prophetic prophecy of the greatest prophet is happiness. Happiness is truly amazing, simply beautiful, perfect harmony in a imperfect World, clarity in the midst of the storm, hope in the midst of tragedy, life after death, a mothers love, a fathers protection, friendship, the light of day, the dark of night, the stars in the sky, rebirth, healing, understanding, epiphany, new relationships, old relationships, peace and love. The prophecy for your life is prophesied and will be fulfilled. Peace and love.

You can never understand me. My life began but it never ended. I was born but never died. I was hated but never loved. I was a friend but never knew a friend. I was a healer but called sick. I was peaceful but only knew war. I was a man but never knew a woman. I was a father but never had a child. I was a good shepherd but never knew a flock. I suffered by the hand of my enemy but never desired revenge, only peace and love.

All glory be to God. God has blessed us all with his holy name. We are all forever hopeful, and can never truly fail. Through Christ whom strengthens us everyone has purpose and courage to fulfill it. With peace and love for all brothers and sisters, we are all truly blessed. In the end we will all understand, but until that day, we must all walk by faith rather than sight, guided by King Jesus and blessed by our Father Gods holy name.

———————— •❦• ————————

If I do not understand you we can not be friends that is like peace. Love is knowing that someone needs you and that you have no need for them yet you still treat them as equal, giving them all the respect and dignity that all of Gods children deserve.

———————— •❦• ————————

Everyday will be a good day, like everyday, stay focused in the midst of the storm, remain diligent on your tasks, because life is as fragile as the mind of a child, and tomorrow is not promised. Find joy in today because today is always ". . . the day which the Lord hath made; let us rejoice and be glad in it".

———————— •❦• ————————

The true nature of war is death, while the true nature of peace is life. The choice is yours, I truly only have one choice to make, and that is life. A life of peace and love is what I desire, full of joy and hope. Those things are as precious as any jewel the World holds, or any star in the sky, and must be earned, and cherished, because they truly are not promised.

———————— •❦• ————————

A love lost is like a heart that does not beat, truly heartless.

———————— •❦• ————————

Revenge is for the weak of mind, mercy is for the strong of heart, love is for the kindred spirit, hate is for the misguided soul, war is for the purpose of peace, peace is for the hope of love, the lie is for the destruction of truth, truth is for the resurrection of life, the resurrection of man. God is for everything, all that is his.

———————————————— •❂• ————————————————

Reject your enemy by living a life of peace and love, because power is happiness; so let no man or woman steal your joy.

———————————————— •❂• ————————————————

Today's lesson is tomorrows test. Tomorrows test is today's success. Today's success is tomorrows hope. Tomorrows hope is today's purpose. Today's purpose is tomorrows victory. Tomorrows victory is today's defeat. Today's defeat is tomorrows peace. Tomorrows peace is today's love.

———————————————— •❂• ————————————————

If you were king for a day what would you do? Would you change all the laws that did not benefit the people? Would you free all the sons and imprison all the lawmen? Would you indulge in all the luxuries the World has to offer? Would you rewrite histories past and reshape the future? Would you reveal all the secrets of the universe? Would you start a war or proclaim eternal peace? If you were king for a day what would you do? Answer this question and discover the secrets of war and learn why peace and love is inevitable.

———————————————— •❂• ————————————————

War is easy, peace is difficult. Life is truth, death is the lie. God is Father, and Jesus is King.

———————————————— •❂• ————————————————

"Where there is smoke there is fire.". Where there is knowledge there is power. Where there is life there is hope. Where there is tomorrow there is today. Where there is man there is strength. Where there is woman there is warmth. Where there is child there is joy. Where there is freedom there is purpose. Where there is truth there is understanding. Where there is lie there is hate. Where there is space there is Earth. Where there is Earth there is victory. Where there is you there is me. Where there is friend there is friendship. Where there is Jesus there is God. Where there is peace there is love.

----•—

The sky is blue like water. The sun is yellow like gold. The grass is green like envy, and all the people are colorless like peace and love.

----•—

Cure the mind. Lift up your brother. Love your sister. Walk to your victory. Run from your defeat. Live for today. Give thanks for tomorrow. Grow wiser from yesterday. Travel lightly. Carry no burden alone with Christ who loves you. Leave your worries behind, and ahead find a life full of peace and love.

----•—

If you ask me a thousand times the answer will always remain the same, I love you. Peace. If I see you for the first time and have known you for years that is amazing grace. Love. If you live to win, you will probably lose, because if winning is your purpose once you have won you will have no purpose. Peace. A kiss from the one you love is like a red rose blossoming at the end of a rainbow, with sunshine as your pot of gold, and raindrops as your tears of joy, truly amazing. Love. If you cry, tears will come down your eyes, but if you smile tears will come down the eyes of the ones you love, smile and the tears will wash away your pain. Peace. When you face adversity you grow stronger from the struggle, this I know because the Bible tells me so. Love. In life once your circle is complete there is only one direction left to go, that is straight. Peace. The World is lost in space, when it is found we can all go home to be with our Father. Love. Leave the past behind, but take its lessons with you into the future. Peace. I live forever hopeful for tomorrows to come, but I know tomorrow will only come if I live today. Love. Forgive your transgressors, they are only a product of the lie, before they were, their was only truth, and the truth holds no transgressions. Peace. Know your enemies, because if you do not you will certainly fall victim to their wrath. Love. Look, and do not speak, and the truth will be revealed in what is heard. Peace. Gods gift is eternity, and he who receives it will be eternally gifted. Love. Gods knowledge is a secret to the World, so the World must walk by faith rather than sight. Peace. The most important knowledge is of self, with that you can conquer the World. Love. The only problem that can never be solved is the problem itself. Peace. Your choices can lead you to your victory, or your defeat, the difference is your choice. Love. Give your life to the Lord because the Lord gave his life for you. Peace. Science versus religion is the question, the answer is science versus religion. Love. The lie can never defeat you it can only lead you to the truth. Peace. The truest knowledge a man can tell you is that they are a son. Love. Your core is important but what is more important is your core. Peace. Envision tomorrow, but live for today, that is walking by faith rather than sight; because tomorrow can never be seen only hoped for. Love. The World has one King and his name is Jesus Christ. The World also has one anti-Christ and his name is Satan. The truth and the lie, the friend and the foe, the good and the bad, the wicked and the righteous, the King and the King. Peace. The answer will tell you what the question is, but the question will never tell you what the answer is that is a luxury of space and time. Love. Peace and love.

Peace be like love. Love be like peace. Peace is love. Love is peace. Peace and Love.

Infinite blessings to those whom live, whom give, whom love, whom respect, whom nurture, whom respect, peace and love.

II.

All people are children of God.

In the season of our Father we can rest, our Fathers love will carry us through. Through life we will all live eternally resting in peace and love.

Genesis teaches us that man fell by the hands of woman whom was deceived by a serpent and introduced the World to sin. God had a second plan however for the salvation of man, and he was the plan, and he gave birth to himself, and named himself Jesus Christ the Messiah.

In the beginning their was man, their was woman, and their was hope for the future. They were three and could not be divided. They were pure, innocent, and forever hopeful. In the end their was the Devil, the Devil made what was indivisible, divisible. Three became four and from the four the World knew evil, war, hate, wickedness, jealousy, envy, pain, sorrow, grief, defeat, sin, death. The three that were indivisible became four, easily divided, easily placed at odds. Their purity became tainted, their innocence became guilt, and their hope became despair. In the beginning their were three, in the end their were four, the fifth element is what we now know to be King.

Sin is the knowledge of good and evil, therefore sin is both. A good sin therefore is the death of evil, and an evil sin is the death of good. The sinful equation to positive defeating negative, and negative defeating positive equals to defeat. Therefore sin is defeat, and the antithesis of sin is victory, something yet to be known by man. The true King is victorious however, not because he defeats sin, but rather for his forgiveness of the sinner.

Cain slew Abel and Abel let Cain live, so it is true you are your brothers keeper! Cain became cursed and Abel became a martyr, so it is true you are your brothers keeper! Cain kept his brother by being cursed and Abel kept Cain by cursing him, so it is true you are your brothers keeper! Keep your brother from the curse.

God tells the Devil the truth, simply saying, "You are not me.".

The greatest reward for God would be for the Devil to love him; God however does not play dangerous games so he asks nothing from the Devil.

Our God can make sense of the senseless; therefore bring your problems to God as your past gives your present a future, like a mother gives her child life, like the sun brings the World light, as the night gives man peace, like King Jesus gave his life for yours.

It is not complicated with our Father God, "Prayers go up, and blessings come down.".

———— •❂• ————

There is no ending, there is only a beginning. Fear no man, for mans power is limited to his time here. Only fear God, for Gods power is endless.

———— •❂• ————

Gods kingdom encompasses us all; there is nothing but the kingdom of God. He sent his only begotten son to save the World and gave him the name Jesus Christ of Nazareth, the Messiah, the only true King. Gods kingdom encompasses us all and Jesus stands at the center, as the only true King.

———— •❂• ————

Try not to worry sometimes you have to ask God twice.

———— •❂• ————

God has never lost, and will never lose. Truth is, that is knowledge. Knowledge is hope. We are all branches that grow from the Tree of Life; therefore everyone is forever hopeful, because God will never lose, and we can never be lost.

———— •❂• ————

I believe that our God is not a poet, a skilled scribe, a masterful artist, a brilliant musician who composes beautiful music and lyrics, but rather that which inspires such creativity that which is simple truth.

———— •❂• ————

Every example of Gods love can easily be understood by the things we understand to be sinful. Every other example only exemplifies things that divide, truly one in the same, truly a vice of the Devil.

———————————•●•———————————

Is it mean that the Devil is traveling on a backward path, standing in the way of righteous progression? Or is it mean that Gods children are not?

———————————•●•———————————

Jesus suffered the most by the hands of the people he came to save. He gave his life so that no one should ever die, but rather be promised the hope of eternal life in Heaven above. Jesus was the Prince of Peace and lives forever through those whom believe in him, and worship his holy name, with a promise to return, and walk eternally through glory with all of Gods children, forever and ever.

———————————•●•———————————

Our Father God is miraculous, he gave birth to himself, and named himself Jesus Christ the Messiah.

———————————•●•———————————

The Prince of Peace wore a crown of thorns and was crucified on a wooden cross at Calvary surrounded by criminals . . . The irony of the story is that Jesus is the Prince of Peace.

———————————•●•———————————

The same blood that ran through Jesus' veins runs through us all, though we are not King, we are all Gods children and possess infinite potential to do good, and hold the hope of the future with in us. The possibility in every man and woman is unknown like the beginning and the end of time an eternal mystery only to be solved by the truth that comes in time. We are all special reflections of that which is true.

The evil that men do is only as a result of the Devils vice, which leads us on a path of self destruction, rather than peace and love.

———— •●• ————

Success is a true blessing from the Lord, but never forget from whence you came because you may just return. Respect the past, live in the present, and pray for the future.

———— •●• ————

Trust in the Lord he will never fail you. Put your faith in that which is true, rather than that which is a lie. God is truth. Give your life to God and the truth will set you free from all the shackles that bind you. Father time is the greatest warrior. Look to your elders for wisdom, and give them respect, they have passed the test of time, and have earned it. Teach the children the way of the Lord and they will change the World. Obey the laws of the land whilst wisdom evades the mind and you will be free until the day it is found. Live for today, and pray for tomorrow.

———— •●• ————

That which is fated by the Lord no man can change, alter, or deny.

———— •●• ————

Paradise is with in so we are all forever hopeful and the prophetic prophecy of Christ is fulfilled. Everyone is promised paradise. It escapes our grasp only as a result of our lack of knowledge of self which is the Devils vice that which keeps everyone from themselves and one another.

———— •●• ————

Jesus promised everyone paradise, therefore if you believe in Jesus you will be destined for paradise. It is promised.

———— •⦿• ————

Christ did not prey on his enemy, he prayed for his enemy.

———— •⦿• ————

Life has no result but death with out Christ. With Christ your life equals to absolute victory. Absolute victory is life after death and life before death. Through Christ our days are multiplied and our time can never be divided. A fraction of our existence is spent searching for Christ, but the answer is with us the whole time. Half of our being is with God, the other half is with the Devil, Christ stands at the center giving us shelter from the storm, and hope in times of hopelessness, in the never ending war between good and evil. A straight path through the circumference leads us to the Father were we join the eternal battle for the salvation of all men.

———— •⦿• ————

Without Christ life is like a contradiction, you live to die. With Christ life is everlasting, eternal, never ending, forever and ever, truly hopeful.

———— •⦿• ————

If their were only one answer and many questions that would be a mystery to some, but to the faithful of heart, who may not know much, and may have many questions, the answer will always be the Lord.

———— •⦿• ————

There is no loser in the eyes of the Lord, there is only the lost and the found.

———— •⦿• ————

Jesus Christ knew the best of the worst, and the worst that knew Christ, knew the best. The mathematics of the relationship is that Jesus knew two, while they only knew one.

The Devil is a fallen angel from Heaven above that truly is the only knowledge that we need of him.

The Devil is a fallen angel from Heaven above blessed with all the knowledge of creation and eternity. He is the enemy of all that is good and pure, the antithesis of life, the personification of death, evil, all that is un-holy. The only reason for his being is hate. The Devil is a cancer to the World, destroying everyone and everything from with in, yet God does not hate the Devil because God knows no hate only love. God is love, and God loves the Devil because his hate is everything his love is not, and understanding the Devil will lead you to a true understanding of his love.

The Devils weakness is that he truly believes he is truth; this is the foundation of his lie. His power and his weakness is the lie, while the truth he holds only exists in our belief in him. The birth of a true King is the only answer to the problem that is the Devil that we know because the Bible tells us so.

The Devil is so clever he will speak to you in Gods voice. Be faithful, steadfast, and determined to win because the war is for your soul. March on children of God, with love as your armor, and peace as your weapon, march . . . , march . . . , march!

The Devil can never win the race because he is going the wrong way. Follow the Lord and you will always win the race; because Jesus is the way. Dreams will be made reality, their will certainly be peace and love awaiting you at the finish line. What way would the lord lead you but to a righteous path to victory. It may be a difficult journey, as the Devil will oppose your every move until the very end. Trust and believe however that in the end he will surely be but a distant memory in the race to glory on the wings of Christ.

The Devil has no knowledge of self and he would hope for us all to be the same. One must shape their identity through the eyes of Christ the King, and search for knowledge of self, and be freed from the evil that would hope to destroy us.

The Devil has never had a fight, yet in still he is the personification of evil. Christ never knew peace, yet in still he is the personification of good. The choice will forever be yours.

The Devil understands, the Devil however understands backwards. He hears what is said before it is said, he understands before it is understood. The Devil is unnatural, unholy. His knowledge and wisdom were given to him by God but it is distorted because he rejected his Fathers love and fell from grace. Fear not however, because the Devil has no power against the children of God. God has written all things from left to right, a straight path to his kingdom, forward rather than backwards, the way of the Lord, the only way to the Father.

The Devil can never be King, because he is hateful; he hates everyone and everything including himself. Live for him who created you, rather than for him whom would wish to destroy you.

The greatest punishment for the Devil is no punishment at all. To understand that is to understand Gods love.

The Devil is the ruler of the underworld, the king of wickedness, the grim reaper himself, evil, yet he too has followers, disciples. Jesus however gave his disciples ". . . the bread of life.". Jesus gave his followers the knowledge of life and eternity, truth. The Devil gave his disciples the knowledge of hate, envy, lust, greed, gluttony, sin, evil itself, the lie. Jesus loved his disciples, while the Devil so hates them whom follow him that he gives them no knowledge of truth, yet in still he tells them they are the truth, and gives them his unholy name, as a curse to their life.

God gave the Devil just what he desired, he gave him the World, everything else he left for Jesus to reclaim. Truth is, all is his, so him who put their faith in the World place their faith in nothing, and them who choose the Lord put their faith in all that their is, and will receive all that Gods kingdom holds. Faithfulness should forever remain with the Lord, because the Kingdom of God holds no hate, only love, no war, only peace and love.

There is no punishment for the Devil. God gave the Devil everything he desired. He gave him the World and all its ways and left everything else for his son, and all that praise his holy name.

The Devil loved God so much he wanted to be God, therefore Gods wrath is not directed towards the Devil himself, rather towards them whom chose him over their Father; therefore the greatest punishment for the Devil is no punishment at all. God lets the Devil live eternal as the lie, which is nothing without the truth, which is him.

The Devil is a fallen angel who wished to fly though God had already blessed him with wings that spanned the length of eternity. Wings that stretched across space and time, as beautiful as the hope of a new day that could take him to heights unknown.

The Devil is the greatest warrior because he is war personified. Jesus Christ is the Prince of Peace because he knows no war, war only knows him. Jesus died by the hands of evil warriors, through his death their was nothing but peace, and after his rebirth their came eternal hope for love.

Confusion is the Devils vice, while clarity belongs to the Lord and all that praise his holy name.

The Devil does not exist, he is only an idea. The idea of his hate is what binds the lonely and lost souls of the World. Be forever faithful. Your enemy does not exist he is only an idea. It is only us that can give him existence. It is your faith and belief in God that is real. Your enemy is only an idea that has no existence with out your belief.

What is turned on by the Lord can never be turned off by man.

—— •◉• ——

One thing is certain; everyone will have problems, whether young or old, black or white, rich or poor, big or small, short or tall. We will all have problems. Solutions however are reserved for those whom call upon the Lord, and praise his holy name.

—— •◉• ——

Yesterday is yesterday, today is today, tomorrow is tomorrow, but forever is like nothing else whilst walking with the Lord.

—— •◉• ——

Destruction and calamity our forever present they reside in the air that surrounds us. Salvation and deliverance however are embedded in our mind, soul, and body, our very being; therefore all of Gods children are forever hopeful.

—— •◉• ——

It is difficult to teach a man whom comes from nothing because their truth is not like most. If you were however to come across such a lost soul introduce them to the Lord. Tell them that Jesus Christ also came from humble beginnings and ran with all sorts of the worst kind. Tell them Jesus denied that truth however, and searched for the true meaning of life and found purpose in us all, promising everyone a better life through his Father. Jesus is the Son of Man, the child of God, the only true King, tell them that he is their friend, and will never deny them.

—— •◉• ——

Christ loves his disciples, the Devil hates his. The choice will forever be yours.

—— •◉• ——

In a World of sin their can only be one answer, one question. The answer can only be Christ, and the question can only be you. A wise man once said, ". . . the answer is like the question because the result leads you to a solution.", this is true like rain drops are blue, and sun beams shine bright like the eyes of a child. The question is will you seek the answer, and the answer will free us all from the World of sin we live in. We are all the question, and the answer will forever be awaiting us.

It is the day that develops my discipline. It is the night that rejuvenates my spirit. It is the World that humbles me. It is the life that brings me joy. It is my family that gives me purpose. It is God that blesses me. It is Christ that forgave me. It is the Devil that makes me stronger, but it is King Jesus the Christ the Messiah whom gives me strength.

Never go to war with a warrior, that is what they live for, that is what they know, that is who they are, and that is their purpose. Be not afraid however everyone has a warrior spirit inside them. Choose a peaceful path however and you will defeat any known warrior, because what is life without purpose. You will then be known forever as a peaceful warrior in the eyes of the Lord.

May God bless all the soldiers who fight for the freedom of all people and watch over them safely until the day they return home. May God bless all people in search of peace and love and give them true knowledge of both so they know once it has come. May God bless the dead and the living alike, because through his son we are all forever hopeful to be as one in Heaven above. Amen, amen, amen.

III.

Discover the life that is yours . . .

———— •❦• ————

Another day gone by what a blessing to have Life! Life is full of lessons some hard, some easy, but all necessary to become the person that God has destined you to be. Give thanks for the lessons learned and look to tomorrow with the hope that a new day brings.

———— •❦• ————

Each day is like a new beginning, a new opportunity for success. It is true you can never forget the failures of the past, you must learn from them; but truth is, you must appreciate the hope that a new day brings.

———— •❦• ————

Every tomorrow is as a result of every yesterday.

———— •❦• ————

Inspiration is everything, it is both the truth and the lie. Inspiration is what helps define us; it is what happens at birth and at death. There is no lie in that which inspires, that which is inspirational, that which inspiration is. When I look to the sky I see peaceful harmony, while some see may hopelessness and despair. When I envision love I see forever, while some may see yesterday. When I catch sight of war I dream of peace, while some continue to live the nightmare. When I awake I pray for better days, while some may wish for more heartache and pain for the people. When I speak to the Lord I cry out, while some may softly whisper his holy name. Inspiration is everything, it is truly innocent, it is him that is inspired that holds the guilt.

The rewards in life are not always happiness and joy, but sometimes rather heartache and pain. The difference is, they both cure you of · your ignorance of Gods love.

The only casualty of victory is defeat.

Life has no imitation. Each life is special and purposeful with meaning at birth and death. In time we can all lose our way, but through amazing grace each wretched soul can be saved! The imitation of life is like a flightless bird, a lost soul, a fallen angel. Life can not be imitated like love can not be duplicated, like sincerity can not be insincere, like kindness can not be unkind, and how trust can not be mistrust. Life has no imitation it is unique, original, special, with no imitation. To imitate life would be like imitating God, and to imitate God is to be the Devil, and the Devil is the antithesis of life, which is our path to the Father, our path to salvation; thus any imitation would be tragic, and thusly lead us to tragedy.

Life with out hope is hopeless. Death without triumph is triumphant. Today without purpose is purposeless. Tomorrow with out yesterday is the end. A friend without friendship is an enemy. A moment without clarity is meaningless. Peace without love is truly impossible.

Every beat of the heart is like a beautiful note in the musical of life.

———————————•❦•———————————

Each beat of the heart is like a moment in time that has been given to us, to reach our destiny, to fulfill our dreams, to discover our purpose, to live joyfully, to be loved, to grow stronger, to gain knowledge, to understand self, to achieve perfection, to inspire truth, to have life.

———————————•❦•———————————

There are truly only two choices in life, one can choose victory, or defeat. The question is what choice will you make, which path will you take. In life nothing is promised except victory or defeat. The choice will forever be yours.

———————————•❦•———————————

In the game of life it is not about who goes first but rather about who goes last.

———————————•❦•———————————

In the game of life there is a passer and a receiver. There is a fumble and a recovery. There is a score and a score keeper. There is a coach and a player. There is a team and a uniform. There is a field and a play. There is a crowd and an arena. There is a foul and a penalty. There is a career and a retirement. There is practice and implementation. There is a professional and a rookie. In the game like in life there is winner and a loser, so life truly is "like a game.", in the game however, the winner wins the game, in life the winner wins life, a victory that knows no end.

———————————•❦•———————————

You have lived through it and learned, been tested and passed, been defeated and gotten up, struggled and overcome, been sick and God has made you well, you have cried and smiled again, you have known sorrow and found your joy. You know have arrived and are ready to reclaim all that you have lost all that has been stolen from you. Your life's trials have taught you, you now know all the rules, all that is left for you to do is to live by them; but regardless I will always love you.

When things are well, and you are set back, do not fret the Lord is always with you that is just his way of letting you know that your journey has not ended; and there are more tests to pass, obstacles to overcome, lessons to be learned.

Wisdom is inherently yours but it is not promised, it eludes us, it escapes our grasp, it is hidden from our sight, it resides behind tomorrows yet to come. One must search for the wisdom that will guide them through the life, the wisdom that will mold the mind and shape the destiny. As each day passes you grow wiser, wisdom is like a seed that grows inside us, watered by life, and time.

Some people are fascinated with evil genius that is clearly evident in the World we live in; me however, I am fascinated with average goodness that requires much more intelligence.

Every person is special and has a name given to them by the people whom love them the most, their parents. The name you are given is a gift to you from your family, and you are a gift to them from God. Sometimes with the evils of the World however, we tend to lose our way, but one thing will always remain certain, family is forever, and forever is Gods gift to us all.

Conflict should only lead to resolution. One should always work to avoid conflict, however if it is inevitable, pray for resolution.

———— •❦• ————

A loser tends to have nothing to lose, so once you have won you must change your life.

———— •❦• ————

One must definitely face defeat, so that one can certainly understand victory.

———— •❦• ————

We are shackled by our adversary and set free by our atonement. Break the chains that bind the mind, soul, and body. Free your self from that which keeps you from your happiness. Happiness is power; it is like a sword to the evils of the World, it is like a cure to the pain. Free you self from that which binds you. Find hope in the simple things, a summer day's breeze, a peaceful moment of silence, a mid-days rest, a smile from a friend.

———— •❦• ————

Sometimes in order to have a perfect day one must have an imperfect one, then one will certainly understand perfection. It is the imperfect day that haunts us, and that gives us purpose, like a father in search of a son, or a warrior in search of peace. It is the imperfect day that defines us as men, perfectly imperfect. Like a star that does not shine in the sky, or a sun that does not set, or a bird that does not fly, or shelter that does not shelter you from the storm, or a prayer that goes unheard, or a friend that does not have a friend, or a mother who has no child, or teacher who does not teach. It is the imperfect day that lets us all know that defeat is possible, but victory is perfection.

———— •❦• ————

All things that begin will eventually end except for that which is forever.

———— •❧• ————

Sometimes the further away you are from the ones you love, the better you can see them.

———— •❧• ————

If you never try you can never succeed. If you are afraid to fail, you may always pass, but you can never say your are fearless; therefore always try to succeed, never fail, but never fear the possibility.

———— •❧• ————

A rose that grows from concrete is like a symbol for hope. If a rose can come from concrete, so can happiness from despair, triumph from tragedy.

———— •❧• ————

If a tree falls in the forest, and no one hears, or sees it, did the tree ever fall? Some may say yes, while others may say no. The truth is like both, so yes the tree did fall with no witness to it, and no the tree did not fall, because no one witnessed it; therefore the answer in life is the witness. Who has witnessed your life, your story, your testimony, none but God can truly testify to your truth. Therefore in life one must walk with the Lord, talk to the Lord, give your life to the Lord, and you will forever be innocent, with the greatest witness of all, to testify to your truth.

———— •❧• ————

If you are serious about your future you will learn from your past.

———— •❧• ————

Learn from your past failures saying, "Never again, not today, not tomorrow, not ever.".

———————— •❦• ————————

Having a heart makes the soul happy, thus being heartless must make the soul sad.

———————— •❦• ————————

Every time you get up you shame the Devil. Every time you get up you give glory to God. Every time you get up you come closer to your dreams. Every time you get up purpose is fulfilled. Every time you get up some one in the World has a friend. Every time you get up you defeat an enemy. Every time you get up you define hope, and redefine hopelessness. Every time you get up you have life! Get up, because from dust we came, but from dust we do not have to return. Our destiny is above and beyond, here, and now.

———————— •❦• ————————

Past failures will never keep one from future success; they are the reason for them.

———————— •❦• ————————

If you are afraid to lose you will never win.

———————— •❦• ————————

You are faced with troubles daily, yet you prevail. You are burdened with problems, yet you resolve. You are cursed by circumstance, yet you remain. You are disrespected, yet you stand tall. You are victimized, yet you stay calm. You are left behind, yet you trail blaze. You are falsely imprisoned, yet you remain free. You are shunned by the people, yet you love the people. You are a survivor, yet you welcome death, because you have survived.

———————————•❂•———————————

If you never fall down, you can never get up.

———————————•❂•———————————

If a man stands on a bridge and looks down a man may contemplate jumping if a man is in pain. If a man stands on a bridge and looks up a man will definitely pray to the heavens above if a man is in pain, therefore a man should always keep their head up. Better days are promised.

———————————•❂•———————————

What is mine is mine. What is yours is yours. What is ours is his. Amen

———————————•❂•———————————

In life there are two tests but only one failure. You can live or you can die, the only failure however is death.

———————————•❂•———————————

Let the light of the Lord clear your vision like a crystal clear nights sky the Lord will guide you through the darkness to the light of a new day. As the World turns we are all forever lost in space, the Lord will forever be our hope, map, and our guide till the day we are found. Each breath we breathe brings us closer to death Jesus' love is breathless and brings us closer to life. Jesus is "life itself" if you live he is your King, if he is your King you will have eternal life. Together we will win, apart we will lose, with Jesus we are together even when we are apart, so we will never be defeated, and will be forever hopeful.

———————————•❂•———————————

Every new beginning is the end of something old. Every ending is the beginning of something new. Renew the mind and you will end your pain.

Hope is like the light at the end of the tunnel. Despair is like a mirage in a desert oasis.

A lost love can never be found but when you find love it can never be lost. Every fighter will lose a fight, but a true fighter will never lose the fight. Everyday will end, but everyday will never end. Every gift has a giver, but every giver does not have a gift. All things come and go, but all things do not come and go. Each person is as valuable as each person, their value however depends on each person. These things I know because the Bible tells me so.

The idea of defeat is scary, but the reality of victory is fearless.

Imagine your worst nightmare becoming your greatest dream come true, and you will understand salvation. Imagine your life after you have lost what can never be replaced, and you will understand defeat; but imagine your life after you have lost what can never be replaced and you will understand victory. Always keep faith, because faith will always keep you. A punishment from God is like a kiss from a friend before your crucifixion. For every good deed there is as equally a dastardly act done that is balance which defines us all. A friend will come only when they have been sent to you, everyone else is like dust in the wind. The purpose you serve will serve you purposely. If you see what is not their you will be considered crazy, but if you believe in what is not their you will be forever hopeful. These things I know because the Bible tells me so.

A lesson is a blessing in disguise, a test is preparation for the blessing that the lesson provides.

Today represents tomorrow simply because today leads us to tomorrow. Be a leader and you will be as today, and represent the people and lead them to tomorrow.

A rainy day can wash away the pain, but a sunny day will dry your tears.

What goes up like the sky and comes down like the Earth? Nothing. So do not say anything and you will be forever innocent of blasphemy. What word means love, and hate? God. Truly amazing, truly everything, truly. Where can you find something that is lost? The mirror. Find yourself right where you stand. Who designed the World? No one, the World designed itself, God designed everything else. Who gives and receives? The giver. Give your life to the Lord and you will receive life. Where can you see the sun but not the sky? In the sky. Like an eclipse of the World Christ came to us.

When you slip and fall their may not always be someone their to help you up, but when you slip and fall there will always be a lesson learned that will help you up.

I have never known much about philosophy, but I do know that when I see a friend I feel safe. When I fall I feel weak, but when I get up I am stronger from the fall. The sun warms my body, but a kiss from a loved one warms my heart. When I cry tears, they dry my eyes, like the truth freeing me from the lie I truly understand Heaven and Hell. Each new day is the same as each new day, but each new day is not the same as each new day. The night is black, and the day holds every color, like a peaceful nights sleep I awake to a puzzle only to be solved by the one who sees no color, only peace and love. Like a blind man philosophy holds no truth, only the hope of sight which will guide us through life.

A blind man can not see, but a blind man has vision, because vision is different than sight. Sight is the perception of images; vision is the perception of faith. Envision yourself as you would want to be, and your faith will see your vision through.

Life is like a game of building blocks, all the pieces are interchangeable, how they come together depends on the builder.

The lawn must be watered in order for the grass to grow, as a man must fall in order to know the fall, as the World must turn in order for us to evolve, as a child must be loved in order to know love. Water your lawn, what your lawn is, is what you envision, what it will become, depends on what you water it with.

If you live for success then you will certainly perish from failure; therefore live for both, because both are equally purposeful in the entirety of ones life. If you live for money then you will certainly perish from poverty; therefore live for both, because they are both equally rewarding from the strength gained from the struggle.

———•●•———

Fall back, let the Lord carry you. The lessons that will be learned are pride, trust, humbleness, friendship, mercy, respect, faith, peace and love, and how to carry on.

———•●•———

No matter how hard you cry you can never erase the pain, but when you cry all the pain will be washed away. Let tears fall from your eyes, feel no shame, man, woman, or child. The tears are like raindrops from the sky that quench the thirst of the World. They are produced from your pain, but your pain is not produced from them. Cry from your pain, and, joy alike. In the end you will be free from the sorrow, so they are both truly the same.

———•●•———

Change can be overwhelming, prepare for it, and brace yourself, but do not fret however, a change will come. That is unchangeable.

———•●•———

When you are free, nothing can imprison you. When you are imprisoned, nothing can set you free except freedom. The difference is freedom is free, and imprisonment can cost you your freedom. Free yourself from that which you pay with your life.

———•●•———

Prepare for your destiny, because your destiny is prepared for you.

———•●•———

If the children are the future, and the elders are the past, who is the present? The answer must be both, and them whom receive the present are the gift.

———— •❦• ————

Pace yourself because tomorrow is only an idea with out today's hope.

———— •❦• ————

The greatest day of ones life I would suggest must be their birth date. The reason being, is that the birth date represents the beginning of ones life, the beginning of ones story. The birthday signifies victory, hope, truth, reflection and perception, contemplation and revelation, genius, wisdom, knowledge, faith, perseverance, determination, courage, celebration, responsibility, struggle, joy and pain, the beginning and the end, wealth, excitement, peace and love, life eternally. Truly the greatest day of ones life, the day it began, and never ends.

———— •❦• ————

If you fall down you can hurt yourself, but when you heal you will be stronger from the fall; therefore I suggest, pray for the fall and let the healing be your blessing, and when that comes you can truly say, "I am blessed.".

———— •❦• ————

Where there is the down trodden their will certainly be them who hold high rank. What separates the two is one is down, and the other is up. Look to Heaven above and you may see the down trodden, while the Devil may hold those of high rank.

———— •❦• ————

If you believe you will achieve, if you have achieved you have believed.

IV.

A wise man once said, ". . . what reward is it to gain the World if you lose your soul in the process?". I agree, so I say reject the ways of the World, and all its temptations. Forge a new path, God will provide all that you need, and fulfill all your hearts desires. All he asks is that you live your life for him whom loved you so much that he gave his only begotten Son to you, to live, and die, so none would ever die again.

———— •●• ————

A wise man once said, ". . . I do not speak much, but I say a whole lot.".

———— •●• ————

A wise man was once asked, ". . . why kind sir do you write peace and love?" the wise man then stands and looks at the other, opening his eyes wide, spreading his arms, opening his heart, and embracing the other man, and simply says, "Because I understand war, and know that that is not the way.".

———— •●• ————

A wise man once said, ". . . though I write about peace and love it can never be said I am a coward. A coward runs from there enemy, I stand firm like the Serengeti against my enemies, with no weapon in hand, but knowledge that my enemy truly has no power over me, but that which is given to them by the Father, in Heaven above.".

A wise man once said, ". . . I can not see quite as well as I used to, I may not catch every word that is said, my body tends not to move quite as fast as it used to, my heart may skip a beat every now and then, thoughts may escape my memory, my wind may not be as good as it was, I may not be up for every challenge; but please do not worry about me because my faith remains as strong as ever.".

A wise man once asked, ". . . what is more foolish, a person whom denies the truth, and lives a lie, or a person whom is a lie, and believes they are the truth?".

A wise man once wrote, "My words our like natures garden, they are organic, they grow in my mind, and blossom on the page.".

A wise man once said, ". . . I am like a sickness to my enemies, there is no refuge from my wrath.".

A wise man once wrote, "The Devils weapon is the lie, take that away from him, and he is powerless against you.".

A wise man once wrote, "My words are as powerful as any weapon of war, but I choose them wisely for the purpose of peace, because I love you.".

A wise man was once asked, ". . . sir what is the Answer?" he then replied, "The answer is the problem and it is not for us to understand because we are not here for understanding, but rather to be understood.".

A wise man once said, ". . . there is no future with out hope, there is no hope with out life, and there is no life without God. So all of time is a like a gift for those whom follow the path of the Lord, and like a curse to them who do not.".

A wise man once said, ". . . the secret to success is that it must remain secret.".

A wise man once said, ". . . I am like a woman, I am impregnated with knowledge, and give birth to truth.".

A wise man was once asked, ". . . kind sir how can the problem be the answer, and the answer be the problem?" The wise man then replied saying, "It is simple, look to the one who is asking the question and you will find your answer. Jesus is the problem and also the answer to the Devil, and the Devil is the problem and also the answer to Jesus, that I give you freely, the understanding is with in your faith.".

A wise man once said, ". . . there is an unnatural relationship between friend and foe. One is the friend and the other is the foe. The simple mathematics of the relationship equals out to nothing ventured nothing gained, absolute zero. In life to truly stand still is impossible, so to be positively a friend, and negatively a foe, and have no forward progress is the antithesis of life.".

———— •••• ————

A wise man once said, ". . . the true nature of revenge is hypocritical. Why seek revenge against someone who has harmed you only to do them harm in return that truly serves no purpose. The true reward comes from forgiveness. Let justice be served by the hands of the Lord, the only true judge.".

———— •••• ————

A wise man once said to his closet friend, ". . . I have a gift, and you my friend are that gift.".

———— •••• ————

A wise man once said, ". . . we are all thoughts before concepts, ideas before reality, lies before truths, defeated before victorious, guilty before innocent, dead before alive, hopeless before hopeful, lost before found, sinners before rebirth. The truth however comes in the end; the beginning is only a reflection of what will be.".

———— •••• ————

A wise man once said, ". . . when you hear no that is your answer, when you here yes that is your question. The answer will always lead you to the question.".

———— •••• ————

A wise man once wrote to another wise man, "Sir I am wise beyond my years because of what I have learned, and what I have taught, and what has come from it. You sir are wise beyond your years because you have learned nothing, and have taught nothing, and nothing has come from it. That sir is wisdom itself, because to be wise is to know nothing but what you know, and have nothing come from it but what is known.".

———•●•———

A wise man once said, ". . . if you live by the lie, you will surely die by the truth.".

———•●•———

A wise man once said, ". . . if you were to give all your time to someone you loved, would it be a gift, or a gift.".

———•●•———

A wise man once said, ". . . defeat is always a possibility, but victory is possibility.".

———•●•———

A wise man once said, ". . . if you were to die tomorrow, would you live today? The answer is no, because to live to die, is not living at all.".

———•●•———

A wise man once said, ". . . if you fail to plan you are planning to fail, therefore plan to succeed and you will never fail, because failure is lack of preparation, and preparation is a plan for success which prepares you for your failures. When you plan to succeed and fail you have not failed at all because your plan was to succeed, and that will never change.".

———•●•———

A wise man once said, ". . . if your sadness is your happiness then no man, or woman truly has power over you except the Father above, and King Jesus whom walks with us all through life and beyond.".

———— •❦• ————

A wise man once said, ". . . the name of life is beginning. The name of death is ending. The ultimate question is, what will your name be.".

———— •❦• ————

A wise man once said, ". . . in the land of my enemy I can not be defeated, the only possibility is victory, because I have knowledge of their truth, which is their name and their eternal punishment.".

———— •❦• ————

A wise man once said, ". . . every time you look to the sky you see the stars, but every time you look to the sky the stars are not there. The truth is, the stars you see only exist if you believe in them. This truth gives man absolute power over man, and we must all forever believe in the stars.".

———— •❦• ————

A wise man once wrote, "I am only a figment of my imagination, and when I imagine myself, I envision tomorrow, which makes me real today.".

———— •❦• ————

A wise man once said, ". . . I have never lost in life because I only believe in winning, not like ignorance, but rather like Gods perfect plan for my life.".

———— •❦• ————

A wise man once said, ". . . if you choose to win you can never lose. Life is about choices, what will you choose? This truly is the only question there is.".

———— •❦• ————

A wise man once said, ". . . if you see success you have left failure behind.".

———————————•❖•———————————

A wise man once wrote, "God will show you defeat before he shows you victory. The reason is that their truly is victory in defeat, but certainly no defeat in victory.".

———————————•❖•———————————

A wise man once said, ". . . the better judgment of man can sometimes cloud the better judgment of man.".

———————————•❖•———————————

A wise man once said, ". . . in a World where everyone is king, there truly is but one king, and it is him whom is not king.".

———————————•❖•———————————

A faithful man once said to his friend, ". . . if you save my life I will be indebted to you forever.".

———————————•❖•———————————

A wise woman once wrote, "A light is only as bright as the people it shines on.".

———————————•❖•———————————

A wise woman once said, ". . . sometimes I am so filled with joy that I am a target for pain.".

———————————•❖•———————————

A wise boy once said, ". . . I hate to be alone, because it makes me lonely.".

———————— •◉• ————————

A wise elder once said, ". . . teach your sons to be quiet, and speak when their spoken to, and in time we will see who the future king is.".

———————— •◉• ————————

A wise person once said, ". . . your life is an extension of your death, that is truth because life only exists before death, and death only exists after life. The truth is, life is before death, and there is nothing after life, which makes life forever, eternal, everlasting.".

———————— •◉• ————————

A wise person once said, ". . . I am a work in progress, and progress is my work.".

———————— •◉• ————————

A wise priest once said, ". . . the Devils disciples sold their soul to gain the World and all its splendors, while truth is, all their heart desired, their soul possessed.".

———————— •◉• ————————

A wise preacher once said, ". . . if you live for the Devils hate, then you will certainly perish from Jesus' love.".

———————— •◉• ————————

A wise preacher once said, ". . . if you live for another, then you will surely perish alone.".

———————— •◉• ————————

A good shepherd once said, ". . . you hate me because you can not steal what is mine, because it is God given, but I love you, so I share what is mine with you freely, wanting nothing in return.".

------ •❂• ------

A wise old prophet once said, ". . . I know nothing but truth, so I walk by faith, rather than sight, through the land of Sodom and Gomorrah, with no knowledge of their ways, only knowledge of my faith that God will guide me home.".

------ •❂• ------

A prodigal son once said, ". . . I am prodigal because I am lost, but I am forever hopeful to be found, because I am a son.".

------ •❂• ------

A wise shepherd once said, ". . . your fear only exists because of the Devil, therefore denounce his existence and you will forever be fearless.".

------ •❂• ------

A wise under shepherd once said, ". . . the Devil is in the pulpit and he preaches the gospel to lead Gods children.".

------ •❂• ------

A wise under shepherd once preached a sermon, he said, ". . . the Devil is the truth because we truly live in Hell, therefore the wrath of God is against his people, not because he hates them but rather because he loves them; because they represent the truth.".

------ •❂• ------

A wise under shepherd once wrote the truth and told lies because he believed in Heaven and Hell.

------ •❂• ------

A wise under shepherd once said, ". . . I can not attend church alone because it is governed by the Devil, but while incarcerated I am as safe as a baby in the arms of Jesus himself.".

A wise old slave once said to his son, ". . . I was beat but I was never beaten. I was knocked down but I was never knocked out. I was whipped but I was never whipped. I was enslaved but I was never a slave.".

A wise slave once said, ". . . there is nothing my masters can do to break me, I am unbreakable.".

A wise uncle Tom once said, ". . . it is true I am an uncle Tom so I can never truly lead black people. I can however speak for white people that truth makes me the leader of both black and white people alike.".

A poor soul once said, ". . . I have lost all that I have had, there is nothing left for me but the Lord, therefore I truly have lost nothing at all.".

A wise failure once said, ". . . when you fail believe that God is watching, so please believe that your failure is purposeful, and can be overcome; because to fail does not mean you are a failure, but rather a precursor to your success. I consider my self a failure because I have successfully achieved wisdom, and am a failure.".

A wise bum once said, ". . . I am poor because I am a bum, but I am not a bum because I am poor.".

A foolish man once wrote, "I am the reason people feel smart, but they are the reason I am nobodies fool.".

A wise don once said, ". . . every man holds truth, but every man does not hold on to it.".

A wise don once said, ". . . I have too much knowledge to be stupid, and I am too knowledgeable to be to smart.".

A wise don once said, ". . . respect an unlawful lawman, until the day it is time for an unlawful lawman to respect the law.".

An evil genius once wrote, "I know nothing but what I have been taught by them whom call themselves innocent, so I believe I am innocent as well.".

A wise poet once wrote, "Poetry is the language of the deaf like love is the bond that binds us all. Beautiful irony.".

A contemporary scholar once said, ". . . science fiction tends not to be fiction at all.".

A wise philosopher once said, ". . . never argue with a fool, because that would be foolish.".

A wise mathematician once said, ". . . it is simple mathematics that govern us, you and me equals we.".

A great thinker once wrote, "To go first and finish last is the same feeling as to go last and finish first. Both paths travel equal distances to their destiny.".

A wise writer once said, ". . . my failure is God written, and my success is God written, therefore I will never fail.".

A wise philosopher once wrote, "Your enemy is on your right and left side. They are on the right standing in opposition of your path to victory, and they are on the left redefining the path which leads to your victory.".

I wise philosopher once wrote, "It is true the truth will set you free, but it is truer that the lie will keep you free.".

A wise Spartan once told his son, ". . . your fear is Persia, a land of mystics, but fear not my son, they too have fear; their fear is our faith in God whom strengthens us, and leads us to victory.".

A wise Spartan once said, ". . . we live by the truth, and we die by the lie, therefore we are eternally Spartans, eternally Sparta!".

A wise physicist once said, ". . . in school I studied the energy operatives, in life I live by the them.".

A wise sex therapist once said, ". . . a woman always desires sex, so if they reject your sexual advance that is a truth a man can build on to meet their mate.".

A wise sex therapist once said, ". . . the psychology of sex is bi-polar you go up and down.".

A wise scholar once said, ". . . when you understand that you are imperfect you will understand Gods perfect plan for your life.".

A wise poet once said, ". . . the moon and the stars are like family and the sun is prodigal and when he returns their will be no darkness, only light.".

A wise business man once said, ". . . customer service should be a service for the customer, not a service for the customer.".

A wise athlete once said, ". . . I run to stay in shape, and I am in shape so that I can run.".

———— •◉• ————

A professional ball player once said, ". . . I ball because I love the game, but I love the game because I ball.".

———— •◉• ————

A wise rapper once said, ". . . I write about the streets because that's what I know, but I read about Jesus because that is what I want to know.".

———— •◉• ————

A wise poet once said, ". . . the purpose of life is purpose. Discover your purpose and live purposely, and purpose will be fulfilled, and your life will forever be lived purposefully.".

———— •◉• ————

A wise philosopher once said, ". . . in life their truly is no straight path, but in the end you will see that nothing truly stood in the way of your destiny.".

———— •◉• ————

A wise scholar once said, ". . . we are all prisoners of fate, even him whom is fated.".

———— •◉• ————

A wise athlete once said, ". . . the last set that you do not want to do is truly the only set you need.".

———— •◉• ————

A wise pianist once said, ". . . each key plays a different note, but each note plays a part in the same song.".

A wise scholar once said, ". . . I am scholarly because I have learned what I have been taught, and I have learned what I have been taught, only because I am a scholar; therefore I was a scholar before I knew, and a scholar after it was known that makes me absolutely a scholar. So to all my friends I say, please call me scholar.".

A wise leader once said, ". . . the people you lead are the reason you are a leader, so if you are a leader lead the people to peace, and in the end you will have love, and will forever be their leader.".

A wise soldier once said, ". . . my journey home begins once I leave for battle, and the battle is not won until my journey is complete.".

A wise soothsayer once said, ". . . never run from the truth, search for it because it is your pot of gold, and never run from the lie, let the truth forever be your shield.".

A wise poet once wrote, "The next level of consciousness only exists if you are conscious of your past level.".

A wise mortician once wrote, "The realm of the living only exists as a result of the living, so be as a ghost, and the realm will be insignificant, and your living will only exist in a realm of significance.".

————— •❂• —————

A wise mathematician once said, ". . . mathematics is logical, therefore if you are logical you are a mathematician.".

————— •❂• —————

A wise scientist once wrote, "Science is a developmental study of natural occurrences which allows man to understand its origins; therefore a scientific study can naturally lead man to the past through the present back to the future.".

————— •❂• —————

A wise poet once said, ". . . the truth about poetry is that there is no truth in poetry. The poetic word is a figment of our imagination, what is real is truly the question.".

————— •❂• —————

A wise poet once wrote, "The nature of a poets mind is neither here, nor there, it is like an idea with no beginning, nor ending. A painting with no colors, nor picture. A World that has no peace, nor love. A poets mind is neither here, nor there like a man whom was never created, nor destroyed.".

————— •❂• —————

A wise friend once said, ". . . look at me like you are seeing me for the first time, but speak to me like you have known me forever.".

————— •❂• —————

A wise astrologer once said, ". . . look to your past for guidance, and you will see your future path.".

A wise parent once said to their children, ". . . the truth is the words you hear and the things you see, the lie is everything else.".

A wise archeologist once said, ". . . my archeological searches are a metaphor for my search for truth. I search purposefully, and am blessed with every new discovery.".

A wise teacher once said, ". . . I teach because I love to be taught.".

A wise philosopher once asked, ". . . innocence is truth, therefore guilt must be the lie, what feeling would you search for?".

A wise Indian Chief once said, ". . . do not be a Indian giver, if you give me your friendship please my friend never take it back, and I assure you I will do the same.".

A wise poet once said to their love, ". . . my deepest thoughts are of you, therefore my love, I love you, because you are truly thoughtful.".

A wise actor once said, ". . . the most unbelievable act to take place is to act itself.".

A wise musician once said, ". . . music is like a lie to the righteous ear, and like the truth to the ear that hears righteously.".

————•◉•————

A wise old warrior once said, ". . . I built with nobodies, became somebody, and went after everybody. In the end their were the nobodies, the somebody, and everybody.".

————•◉•————

A wise warrior once said, ". . . their is a war going on and we are the target, but I am safe, because I am alone.".

————•◉•————

A wise warrior once said, ". . . to defeat all of my enemies I had to let some of them go.".

————•◉•————

A wise warrior once said, ". . . I am married to war, and my children are peace, and I have named them love.".

————•◉•————

A wise warrior once said of his enemy, ". . . I offered them peace and they chose war, therefore we are forever in conflict, because to choose what is not offered is torture.".

————•◉•————

A wise warrior once said, ". . . your enemy is a coward, and a criminal, therefore they have no refuge from the law, or the lawless alike.".

————•◉•————

A wise warrior once wrote, "A peaceful attack is impossible to stop . . .".

A wise warrior once said, ". . . the greatest warrior will always choose peace, and subsequently receive love.".

A wise warrior once said, ". . . my mathematics is not right so I choose war. When my math is right I will have peace.".

A wise warrior once said, ". . . the birth of my enemy gave me life, and their death will give me life eternally.".

A wise warrior once said, ". . . my battles prepared me for my battles, and my defeats prepared me for my victories.".

A wise warrior once wrote, "There is no victory in defeat, but there is certainly defeat in victory.".

A wise warrior once said, ". . . all my enemies are the same, there is no difference between them. They all desire the same thing from me, an enemy is an enemy. They are the same as one, two, or three. They have one purpose, and that is my defeat, and one name, and that is my enemy.".

A wise warrior once said, ". . . your enemy is special but they are only special because of you, so give them peace and curse their name. Make them what they are to you, truly nothing.".

A wise warrior once said, ". . . I defy my enemy, when they stop I go, when they say walk I run, when they say surrender I attack, when they say retreat I march on, when they say die I live eternal.".

A wise warrior once wrote, "Your enemy is your friend because they always tell you the truth that they are your enemy. Your friend is your enemy because they always show you the truth, of who your true friend is.".

A wise warrior once said, ". . . I once was in a war defenseless with no weapon, until one day I fell to my knees, and prayed to heaven above. God heard my prayers and answered me, and blessed me with faith, and the knowledge of his love and it has protected me ever since.".

A wise warrior once said, ". . . when I was a prisoner of war I lived amongst my enemy. Now that I am free I live amongst my enemy.".

A wise warrior once said, ". . . the most complicated thing known to man is peace, it has eluded us since the beginning of time; therefore to achieve peace would be the greatest achievement known to man, and the greatest reward would be love.".

A peaceful warrior once said, ". . . my enemy needs me to fight me so I do not give them what they need, instead I give them what I want, and that is peace, and love.".

The jeweler to the king, ". . . with all do respect your royal highness, how can you be king when I hold all the jewels?".

A wise king once wrote, "I can never truly be king because I believe in God. I can however be like the true King, Jesus, and call everyone my brethren.".

A wise king once said, ". . . the only way to defeat me, is to be me.".

A wise king once said, ". . . only follow me who is your king, all others you must lead.".

A wise king once said to the prince, ". . . you my son are my only fear, because one day you will be king and take my throne; therefore my son you now know a true king is fearless.".

A wise king once said, ". . . I am the king so that I can be the people.".

A wise king once said, ". . . I am king, therefore, I am the only true enemy of the king.".

A wise king once said, ". . . my first name is my last name, and my middle name is who I am. The question is what will you call me.".

A wise king once said, ". . . I live among my subjects that I rule, but truth is, I am alone, because I am the only king.".

A wise king once said, ". . . live for yourself but die for your king. The reason being that your king is only your king if you call them king, and if you call them king they will never let you die.".

A wise king once said, ". . . in the game of Chess the pieces do not speak they only move. Life is like the game of chess to the true king, the pieces do not speak, they only move.".

A wise king once said, ". . . honor is nothing more than a word without the honorable.".

V.

The sparkling of the seas reflection appeared in my window pane awakening me to a World of pain and agony with hope outside my window.

The sky is endless. There is no end to the sky, to its beauty, to its splendor. Its glory is it has no ending nor beginning. That is magnificent simply because to exist with no known beginning is like the birth of a King, truly existing through mans belief in him, which brings him eternal, everlasting life. The sky is truly our limit if we only believe.

Leave me alone with the Lord whilst I am sick. I find peace and tranquility in my solitude that is a spiritual healing. As I struggle to regain my health I become closer with my Father, and feel the blood of the Lord healing me. My mind is weakened in an ill state and my body is a curse rather than a gift, a tomb, rather than a great pyramid. Allow me to heal and regain my strength. Pray for me in hopes that I may reclaim my power and all the happiness and joy that comes with it; but leave me alone with the Lord whilst I am sick for when I am well you will be my reward.

I can not live for you, I can not walk for you, I can not talk for you, I can not think for you, I can never cry for you, I can not fight for you, but I will always be for you.

———— •●• ————

The body is mechanical, the soul is spiritual, the mind is mystical, the brain is metaphorical, the family is biological, the wife is beautiful, the seed is generational, the elders are inspirational, the life is hopeful, the time is purposeful, the Lord is magical, our God is all powerful.

———— •●• ————

I am my Gods child, I am my Lords servant, I am my fathers son, I am my mothers baby, I am my sisters brother, I am my nieces uncle, I am my grandmothers grandson, I am my cousins cousin, I am my uncle and aunts nephew, I am my friends friend, and my enemies enemy, I am my selves hope . . . , "I am that I am".

———— •●• ————

The Lord works in mysterious ways. He will give you the answer before he gives you the problem. He knows who you are before you know yourself. He loves you when you do not love yourself. He gives to you when you take from him. He gives you peace when you give him war. He prays for those who are his enemy. He will whisper softly in a World of noise. He will carry you through life, and walk with you through eternity. He will trust his betrayer, and serve his servant. Our lord works in mysterious ways, his love has no meaning yet defines us all.

———— •●• ————

The longevity of Gods love is the longevity of Jesus' reign as King, is the longevity of the suns rays, is the longevity of the Earths life, is the longevity of the stars shine, is the longevity of the moons glow, is the longevity of a roses beauty, is the longevity of deaths loss, is the longevity of life's hope, is the longevity of a child's joy, is the longevity of a mans vision, is the longevity of a woman's nurture, is the longevity of a enemies hate, is the longevity of a friends friendship, is the longevity of wars destruction, is the longevity of peaces resurrection, is the longevity of Gods plan for us all. Forever and a day remain hopeful, it is all a metaphor for "longevity".

———————————•●•———————————

God will teach when it is time to be taught. You will learn when it is time to be learned. You will see when it is time to be seen. You will discover when it is time to be discovered. You will get up when it is time to be getting up. You will understand when it is time to be understood. You will have when it is time to have. You will receive when it is time to be received. You will transition when it is time to be transitioning. You will succeed when it is time to be successful. You will do all things when it is time that is his will, and that will be done when it is time.

———————————•●•———————————

The greatest gift from God is God himself everything else is a blessing. Truth is like painless pain, hate with no animosity. God is like truth to them whom are wicked and to them whom live righteously alike. To speak hate with no hate in a World with no love is the wrath of God and a gift to the righteous and wicked alike. Gods greatest gift is himself, nothing is greater than his holy name, everything else is truly a blessing.

———————————•●•———————————

The Devil is the king of Hell. Jesus is the true King. God is the Father. Cain slew Abel. David defeated Goliath. Judas hung from a tree. Eve tempted Adam. Adam fell to temptation. Sin is the knowledge of good and evil. Life begins at conception. Death ends life. Man takes life. Jesus saves life. Jesus was man. The Devil is a man. God created man. In the end their will only be man.

———————————•●•———————————

Imagine if every time you spoke the future was changed. Would you choose your words wisely? Imagine if every time you moved reality was shaped. Would you move more carefully? Imagine if every time you touched someone they were healed. Would you choose your friends more carefully? Imagine if every time you cried some one smiled. Would you hold back your tears? Imagine if every time you prayed some one was saved. Would you give your life to the Lord?

If it will be it will be. If it is fate it will be fated. If it is love it will be forever. If it is hope it will be hopeful. If it is understood it will be understanding. If it is tomorrow it will have been today. If it is given then it will have been received. If it is destiny it will be destined. If it is a king it will be a kingdom. If it is mine it will be ours. If there is a rule it will be a ruler. If it is imperfection it will be perfection. If it is darkness it was light. If it is rain their will be sunshine. If it is taught it will be learned. If it is a girl it will be a woman. If it is a boy it will be a man. If it is a struggle it will be progress. If it is defeat it will be victory. If it is Christ it will be an answer. If it is God it will be.

The night be like darkness, clarity to the mind, hindsight twenty-twenty, with the days reflection appearing in the mind. A thing of beauty, or turbulent pain? Fear not paradise is promised to all of Gods children, all of Gods faithful of heart.

If you believe in the sun you should believe in the day. If you believe in the stars you should believe in the night. If you see the lie you should speak the truth. If you walk by sight you should live by faith. If you believe in God you should accept Christ as your Lord and savior.

God will give sight to the blind and take sight from those whom fail to see, right. Man will steal from the poor and give to the rich for the purpose of political gain, right. The Devil will wear a mask of the righteous in order to deceive Gods people, right. A person can never know truth yet in still be the truth, right. The World revolves around the sun like the son revolves around the Father, right. Giving up is impossible if a person is destined, right. When you build use bricks of peace and love, anything else would be like a house of cards, right. Left I am on the Right!

———————

Truth is, I do not know you but I do know God, so I know you are special, and we can learn from one another, and build if it is meant to be. Like King Jesus the carpenter we are all builders, and blocks, and have infinite potential to change the World together, if it is meant to be it will be.

———————

A thousand stars shine for one moon, like one sun shines for every person, like one death can save many lives, like one friend can defeat every enemy, like one lesson can pass every test, like one Christ can forgive every man, as one God can create one World.

———————

The Tree of Life grew from the seed of hope rooted in the soil of destiny sprouting leaves of joy and happiness with eternal branches of eternity reaching out to the World to spread truth and knowledge for all of Gods children never to die only to live strong and faithful full of wisdom life hope and truth through all of time.

———————

A new season is on the horizon now. The trees are changing colors now. The grass is seizing to grow now. Animals are migrating now. With a new season we see what is now, and reflect on what was then.

Now is the time to prepare for what will be, what is now, and mend all that has past. Looking up at the sky I see a beautiful oasis of colors illuminating the World shining brightly in my mind like the sun in the sky. Red reflects my life, blue reflects perfection, and yellow reflects my trust in Gods perfect plan for me, so beware because I am a son, but fear not because peace and love is my purpose, anything else is truly the Devils vice. In the new season I declare victory over the past and defeat over all that stands in the way of my future.

—— •●• ——

The suns light shines through my window pane from the beautiful sky above, the stars are hidden by the days light; the moon is but a distant memory. The birds fly high above, the Worlds energy fills my mind, body, and soul, I am alive! The new day is like a mystery waiting to be solved. I arise and breath breaths of peace and love full of life knowing not what the day holds only that I am here and apart of the plan set forth by our Father before the dawn of time. I sit still as my body awakens silently awaiting the truth, no different from any other man, woman, or child of the highest stature, or that of the lowest. We are the same! Are only difference is the part we play in the never ending story that is life.

—— •●• ——

Today has come and gone, tomorrow awaits our arrival, the night is here for us to rest, and prepare for the new days test, hopefully all will pass. Do not fret however, enjoy the time you have. Do what you know is right, and you will never fail. The talents you posses are no mistake, they were given to you to discover, nurture, and use, and can never be taken away. Appreciate what makes you unique and enjoy the day that awaits your arrival.

—— •●• ——

The stars lay across the nights sky sparkling ever so bright, bringing light to the dark, guiding us through the night. The moon sits high above like a father to his son it shines above the stars illuminating the nights sky. It is a simple yet natural beauty that no artist can depict, that no poet can describe, which no man can deny. The nights mystery is the days purpose, the days work is the nights rest, the nights power is our weakness. We are humbled by its beauty, and must be guided through it by the light of the night that shines through the darkness. As our faith guides us through the life so must we all travel through the night.

———————————— •❂• ————————————

Words are like power. The mind is like a garden. The body is like a temple. Knowledge is like the endless sky. Wisdom is like time. Time is like life. Death is like an enemy. An enemy is like defeat. A friend is like love. Love is like trust. Trust is like family. Family is like blood. Blood is like our bond. Our bond is like our savior. Our savior is Jesus. Jesus is like God. God is like nothing else.

———————————— •❂• ————————————

It is ironic to be a jealous king. It is ironic to live for today and die for tomorrow. It is ironic to be a fearless leader. It is ironic to be a under shepherd. It is ironic to cry tears of joy. It is ironic to be ironic.

———————————— •❂• ————————————

Tragedy is tragic only because the successful fall short of success. Only because the righteous are treated un-righteously. Only because the truth is the lie, and the innocent are found guilty. Only because the stars do not shine. Only because the sick are not made well, and the well is always dry. Only because a friend is the enemy, and an enemy is the friend. Only because yesterday knows no today, and today knows no tomorrow.

———————————— •❂• ————————————

Oh what a beautiful day is today, like none before, and like none after. The sun sits high above, shining brightly down on the Earth, on every man, woman, and child. The clouds float ever so gently across the clear blue sky. The birds are singing, hearts are beating, full of life! Our time is ever so precious on a day like today, this is truly the day the "Lord has made.".

———————————— •●• ————————————

If tomorrow never comes, and yesterday is but a distant memory, look to today as a shepherd to his sheep, as a lioness to her cub, a father to his son. Live today as the everlasting fire that burns in the sky, as the stars that shine above, as the clouds that float across the horizon. Live today as if you were a child filled with innocence, and joy, peace, and love, and look to the end as a new beginning, because truth is, tomorrow is not promised, and yesterday is but a distant memory.

———————————— •●• ————————————

I imagine . . . , in a perfect World their would be no need for words, language will be obsolete, silence would be king. We would all share a universal understanding, a collective unconscious, one truth . . . As day transitions to night so would all of Gods creatures move harmoniously through the four seasons of life. Our reflections would be endless moments of epiphany, never to be spoken, only to be felt . . . Like the stars in the sky each soul would illuminate the World, inspiring the mind, shaping our destiny, with words unspoken . . . Like a knife piercing the skin a utterance would be to the peaceful silence that would be king in the perfect World I imagine.

———————————— •●• ————————————

Stand still in the midst of the storm, your movement can lead to your destruction, while your stillness can save your life. There is chaotic confusion in the midst of the storm, and clarity in its passing. Stand still until clarity has come and life will be as it was before the confusion and you will be stronger for weathering the storm.

———————————— •●• ————————————

Oh what a magnificent glorious day awaits tomorrow, filled with infinite possibility only to be revealed in time. To have life, with death always present surrounding us, never to subdue our will or to encompass our existence, only to succumb the wicked of heart that live by hate, never the pure of heart whom live by faith. Never to separate the righteous from the day that awaits tomorrow, filled with the mystery, and marvel of the World, only to be explored by the mind of man whom holds infinite possibility to discover truth, in the magnificent glorious day that awaits tomorrow.

Death chases life, like night chases day, the hunt is on and we are the prey. Deaths relentless pursuit of happiness is an eternal struggle, a never ending battle for life. There is truly no escape for the false of heart, nor the weak of mind. Death will seek and find all that lack the "bread of life", the spiritual nourishment that strengthens us on our journey through time. As Christ above we too can defeat death and find forever on the wings of faith, riding a chariot of destiny, on a path of silver and gold, through life, death, eternity, and beyond.

The beauty of a curse is that it has no beauty. The truth about death is there is no life. The joy about pain is there is no joy. The purpose of destiny is purpose. The hope of a child is hope. The colors in a rainbow are the pot of gold at the end. The reward for victory is defeat. The power of knowledge is powerful. Perfect harmony is perfect harmony. Jesus' crucifixion is sin. Jesus' resurrection is Christ the Messiah from Nazareth the only true King. Gods plan is time, Gods time is timeless, timeless time stands still while everything else moves, so life truly is but a dream.

April showers bring May flowers. May flowers bring new life. New life brings new hope. Hope brings man closer to God. God gives us all purpose. Purpose leads us to understanding. Understanding unites us. Together we atone for all wrong doings. What is right will shape the future. The future depends on the children. We must teach the children what is right. The children will carry the torch, and guide us to tomorrow. Everyone will be together again in Heaven above. All will live forever with our Father God, and King Jesus because April showers brought May flowers.

—————————— •◉• ——————————

Life is like a kaleidoscope, when you open your eyes all the colors and shapes appear.

—————————— •◉• ——————————

Mystical rain drops drip slowly from the sky, cleansing the World of all that is the lie, leaving no trace of what could make a dove cry. From Heaven above our blessings come to help us all survive. Never will it be known who will live or die, so all of Gods children must walk by faith rather than sight like the blind. In the end all truth will be told, and we can all live eternal with King Jesus, through all of time.

—————————— •◉• ——————————

The night brings the day, the day brings the night, together they are everything, apart they are but a dream. A dream that is born in the night and lives in the day is no dream deferred at all, rather a blossom of true beauty, something like tears of joy and songs of peace and love. The night that turns to day, and the day that turns to night, is like the boy who turns to man, the slave who turns to king, the son who returns to the Father, the pain that turns to joy, the life that turns to the Lord. A dream is but a dream, but a dream that is born in the night, and lives in the day is the nights gift to the day, and the days gift to the night, together they are everything, apart they are but a dream.

—————————— •◉• ——————————

A lazy bird can never take flight. A heartless lion can never be king. A faithless person can never lead. A coward can never know peace. A war can never resolve conflict. A soldier can never run from battle. A battle can never be fought in harms way. A person can never get up until they fall down. A flower can never blossom in darkness. A child can never learn without being taught. A man can never know love until they know God. A victory can never be won without a defeat. A woman can never know man until they know Jesus. A problem can never come before the answer. A destiny can never be fulfilled until it is destined. A life can never be found until it is lost. A tree can never grow without water. A story can never be told without a story teller. Never before, what is never.

———•◉•———

A little birdie once told me that the sky was not blue rather clear like the sea, and that the grass was not green rather brown like the Earth and that its color is only a mask from the World, and that the stars did not shine rather sparkle like the eyes of a child, and that the sun did not burn rather beat like the heart of man, and that the moon did not glow rather reflect the souls of the living in memory of the dead, and the little birdie was right, because the little birdie had no sight, only faith, and the Lord, to watch over them and guide them through the life.

———•◉•———

The fall leaves traces of summer rain, with memories of spring blossoms, and winter wonderlands, painting the sky beautiful colors of happiness, and joy; covering the Earth with a dazzling array of browns, oranges, and yellows. Histories past stretches across the land, as the day becomes night the World rests. As the seasons transition in time their will be new life and all that was barren will be anew, and each man, woman, and child can see once more the World that the Lord has made.

———•◉•———

Every star shines bright for every star, like every person lives for every person, like every day exists for everyday, like each birth is because of each birth, like every season is a new season, like all of time is a gift to all of time, like your happiness comes from happiness.

———————————•●•———————————

Let their be light. Let their be night. Let their be day. Let their be tomorrow. Let their be freedom. Let their be freedom. Let their be joy. Let their be abundant joy. Let their be happiness. Let their be peace. Let their be love. Let their be hope. Let their be hopefulness. Let their be imperfection. Let their be perfection. Let their be, let their be, let their be.

———————————•●•———————————

Purpose is purpose. Truth is truth. Life is life. Death is death. War is war. Peace is peace. Hope is hope. Love is love. Hate is hate. Forgiveness is forgiveness. Knowledge is knowledge. Victory is victory. Defeat is defeat. Power is power. Weakness is weakness. Sickness is sickness. Healing is healing. Friendship is friendship. Adversity is adversity. Perfection is perfection. Faith is faith. Evil is evil. Good is good. If something is what it is, then truth is, their truly is no question, only an answer, with no question.

———————————•●•———————————

If ugliness is a curse then beauty must be the cursed. Looking into the World, ugliness can be viewed as beauty, truly a curse that must mean the World is like a curse to them whom live in it, because beauty is true, and we are all beautiful; truly a curse in a World of ugliness.

———————————•●•———————————

A true love comes like a eagle to its pray, like the night to the day, like the rain to the bay, like the light to the shade, like a hero to the afraid, like guidance to the astray. True love is breathless and will sweep you away, and carry you through life, through eternity, and a day. True love is a dove in flight, on a star glistening night, shining ever so bright, illuminating the sky, captivating everything in sight. True love is truly amazing, everything we love, everything want, everything we are, everything we are not.

A woman's love is like no other, it is like the birds in the sky, the moon in the night, the beat of the heart, the beauty of the soul, the beat of the drum, a kiss from above, a warm embrace, the hope of a new day, a rose that grows from concrete, lilies in the field, the joy of victory, the agony of defeat. A woman's love is like nothing else, and should be cherished, truly a gift from above.

What is the measure of a man? Is it his love for God, family, or friends? Is it his degree of tolerance, patience, discipline? Or is it his accomplishments, success, money? Who truly knows the measure of a man, who can truly judge what makes a man a man. Some would say a man is a male of eighteen years of age, which I assume is a small fraction of the truth. Ask any number of people what makes a man a man, and you will most likely get any number of answers. Who truly knows the measure of a man but God, but until the day comes that it is known, I certainly will measure myself against the Lord.

Man is scientific simply because his blood is biological. Woman is physiological simply because her womb carries life. Children are artistic simply because their mind requires molding. Family is romantic simply because it is love that binds them. Heaven is invisible simply because it is there but not seen. Hell is judgmental simply because it sentences you to death. Life is ironical simply because it is death that defines it. Jesus is hopeful simply because his promise to return. God is institutional simply because we are captivated by his holy name. Everything is, simply because everything is, and everything will be, simply because, everything is, simply because.

A blind man can create beautiful art. A deaf man can compose harmonious music. A sick man can heal many wounds. A weak man can lift many burdens. A grey sky can inspire inspirational colors. A true friend can last forever. A true enemy can reveal the truest friend. A single glimpse can spark endless love. A child's smile can illuminate the World. A mother's kiss can mend a broken heart. A bird at flight can calm a restless World. In Jesus' holy name it can happen. Amen

One mans success is another mans failure. One mans victory is another mans defeat. One mans triumph is another mans tragedy. One mans destiny is another mans fate. One mans love is another mans hate. One mans friend is another mans enemy. One mans pain is another mans joy. One mans knowledge is another mans power. One mans hope is another mans despair. One mans freedom is another mans imprisonment. One man is the truth the other man is his truth, be one man.

Questions lead to answers. Answers lead to solutions. Solutions lead to progress. Progress leads to change. Change leads to defeat. Defeat leads to victory. Victory leads to the Lord. The Lord leads to the Father. The Father is God. God leads us all. With God we are all lead through life and beyond.

A battle is fought, won, and lost everyday. Some battle to make it through the day. Some battle to do the simple things, like awake in the morning, make it through the afternoon, to the evening, to the night, to the next day again. Some face other battles, with life, relationships, work, and financial obligations. Others battle on a grander scale, like a true leader, or one whom sustains the people. A battle is a battle however, and the reward which comes is the same for every man, woman, and child, who battle the good battle, and win!

Something with no meaning has no purpose. Something with no purpose has no hope. Something with no hope has no future. Something with no future is the antithesis of life. The antithesis of life is death. Life is the glory, the victory, and the defeat, the peace and the love, the past, present, and the future. Life is everything. Look to the giver of life, receive the gift of life, and give it back, and you will be as the giver, and have life everlasting.

If you only know the title, and no story you truly know nothing. If you only know war and no peace you truly no nothing. If you only know hate and no love you truly know nothing. If you only know destruction and no reconstruction you truly know nothing. If you only know victory and no defeat you truly no nothing. If you only know Jesus and no Christ you truly know nothing. If only you know, you truly know nothing.

If you give you may not always receive, but if you give you will forever be known as a giver. If you are evil, you will still have life, but you will eventually die; but if you are good, you will have life after death. If you put your faith in the Lord, he will never betray you, but if you choose not to, he will still never betray you. If you do the Lords will you will forever be known as a giver, never to be betrayed, through life, death, and beyond.

Do not stare directly into the sun, close your eyes and feel its warmth. Do not listen to doubters, teach fellow believers. Do not give up on your dreams, turn them into reality. Do not lose faith in hard times, find faith in hard times. Do not do, what should not be done, do what you should do. In Jesus' holy name I pray, amen, amen, amen.

––––––––– •●• –––––––––

It is inevitable tomorrow will come, and if it never comes, know that it was inevitable.

––––––––– •●• –––––––––

Imagine yourself free like a bird, and you may soar like an eagle, but imagining your self free like a bird can only take you so high, you must have peace and love. Imagine yourself trapped, and I am sure you can imagine yourself free from the trap with knowledge of the trap as your reward. Imagine you saw a man fall and get up and you will see your imaginations potential. Imagine the imaginations power, and you will know peace and love.

––––––––– •●• –––––––––

Your life is like a calm summer day, or a star glistening night's sky. Like a crystal clear lake stretching across the horizon, as the birds sing and the wise old owl hoots so is your life like a beautiful nights sleep awakened by the hope of a new day.

––––––––– •●• –––––––––

Look to the sky, and find hope for the land that is your home. Nurture the land, and find a home awaiting you in the sky. In the sky there is peace and love that is hope like a map for the World that is our home. Look to the sky, and learn the peace and love that you would wish for the land you call home.

––––––––– •●• –––––––––

Time is the thread that connects histories past, to today's present, to tomorrow's future. Time is the cure for all things. In time you will always see, time gives sight to the blind like a star in the sky guiding a lost ship at sea, time is our map. Time is but limited; it is as precious as the most precious jewel the World holds. Like the Nile in Egypt time is everlasting, flowing eternally. All answers come in time, while all questions come from time. Each moment is but a drop in the sea of time, we all live in, forever and ever.

———— •●• ————

In time all truth will be revealed, thus in time all lies will become what they are, thus all their wounds will be healed, thus peace and love is inevitable, thus we will always be we, and every lost person to violence, hatred, disease, war, sickness, evil . . . , will always have knew life, thusly we can all live eternally as one, through all of time.

———— •●• ————

When the sun rises and the moon is but a distant memory who will be free, only time will tell. After the storm passes and the dust clears who will be standing, only time will tell. When the war is won and all the soldiers return home who will be king, only time will tell. When your journey has ended and you have gained knowledge, wisdom, and victory, what will be your story, only time will tell. After the end when their becomes a new beginning what will be, only time will tell. Only time will tell, what will come in time.

———— •●• ————

If you tell me I can't I will tell you I can. If you tell me to walk I will run. If you tell me to stop I will go. If you tell me to sit down I will stand up. If you tell me a lie I will tell you the truth. If you tell me you hate me I will tell you I love you. If you tell me to lose I will win. If you tell me anything I will do the opposite, but if you ask me we can build and do the Lords will together, because to tell me is to be me, animosity which has defined all wars, while to ask is resolution that defines all peace and love, this I tell you.

———— •●• ————

You and I are the same. Together as one we are strong. Separate as two we are weak. Their once was a struggle between us, now we are balanced, now we can build. You can lead, and I will follow that will define us; because together we will do the impossible as one. No one can deny us, because we are stronger as one, and they are weaker as two. We are together, and they are apart. Our journey begins know that our struggle has ended.

———————————— •●• ————————————

We fell out over love and came together over hate. We started out as everything and ended up as nothing. What we were was amazing but what we became was a tragic. From everything to nothing, from love to hate, from amazing grace, to tragic tragedy, to lose love, and gain hate. Like Genesis we began and like Genesis we ended, all things in between are truly a mystery.

———————————— •●• ————————————

If the question is pain, the answer is pain. If the question is joy, the answer is joy. If the question is love, the answer is love. If the question is hate, the answer is hate. If the question is truth, the answer is truth. If the question is lie, the answer is lie. If the question is me, the answer is me. If the question is you, the answer is you. If the question is us, the answer is us. If the question is forever, the answer is forever. If the question is death, the answer is death. If the question is life, the answer is life. If the question is a question, then the answer must be the question, and the question must be the answer. Truth is, every question answers itself, like everyday answers the question for everyday, and how every question answers the question for every question.

———————————— •●• ————————————

Collectively we are unconscious, unconsciously we are lost, lost we are in search, searching! We are all purposeful; purposefully we are dangerous, danger! Danger awaits us around every turn; turning can lead us astray, astray! Astray means we are guilty; guilt comes to those whom do not follow the righteous path, righteously! Righteously we march to victory; victory is understanding our friend, thus defeating our enemy, enemies! Enemies beware, because your truth has been revealed; truth is, collectively we are unconscious, unconsciously we are lost.

———•◦•———

The hope of the slave is the slave, like the hope of man is a man, like the hope of the World is the World, like the hope of the future is the future, like the hope of our salvation is salvation, like the hope of the truth is truth, like the hope of our destiny is destined, and like the hope of hope is the hopeful.

———•◦•———

I am the hope of the slave, I am like freedom nothing can imprison my spirit. My spirit belongs to the Lord, and he guards it with his life, which is ". . . life itself.", and he feeds it with his love. I know this because I am forever hopeful, this I know because the Bible tells me so. Jesus is the past, the present, and the future, the everything, all their truly is, our hope our salvation for life.

———•◦•———

My heart beats like a war horse racing to battle on the field of glory, warrior above, main flowing in the wind, coat like silver and gold. Each stride is power, the strength of the warrior and the horse are as one courageously charging to victory. My heart is like a war horse, as it beats so does the horse of war race to battle, carrying a warrior to his destiny, to his purpose, to an inevitable fate of peace and love.

———•◦•———

I can never fly like an eagle simply because an eagle flies above the clouds, but I can walk like a man simply because man walks with King Jesus in Heaven above. I can never know you simply because I have not walked in your shoes, but I can understand you simply because I have not walked in your shoes. I can never defeat, defeat, simply because defeat is absolute victory, but I can become victorious simply because victory is absolute defeat. I can never paint a beautiful picture simply because beauty is in the eye of the beholder, but I can tell you what beauty is simply because beauty is in the eye of the beholder. I can never be alone simply because people are like a reward to him who has peace and love, but I can be rewarded with peace and love simply because I am alone. I can never simply because I can never, simply because.

—•—

What is truth but forever. What is a lie but absence of truth. What are you but me. What is the sky but a crown. What is man but king. What is purpose but understanding. What is understanding but genius. What is genius but everything. What is love but peace. What are the stars but amazing. What is the Father but the son. What is the World but a mystery. What is destiny but weakness. What is weakness but lack of power. What is power but absolute. What is absolute but me, you, and God. What is the son but the Father. What burns bright in the sky, and warms the Earth, but the sun. What is the sun but fire in the sky. What is fire but warmth personified. What personifies identifies that which is an idea with that which is real. What is real is what is tangible to the touch; therefore God is not real unless we believe. What is God but our belief in him, and what is, is Gods gift to us all.

—•—

Knowledge with no power, is like power with no knowledge. Life with no hope, is like hope with no life. Progress with no struggle, is like struggle with no progress. A lesson with nothing learned, is like learning with no lesson. A victory with no reward, is like a reward with no victory. A child with no joy, is like a joyless child. A problem with no answer, is like an answer with no problem. Today with no tomorrow, is like tomorrow with no today. Heaven with no Earth, is like Earth with no Heaven. God with no love, is like death with no life, truly an impossible possibility.

———— •❖• ————

I can tell you the meaning of all things if you will only listen. I can tell you why their should be three dots rather than four at the end of your continuous thought. I can tell you why the sun sets in the east, and rises in the west, why the birds sing, and the doves cry. I can speak with you for hours on why the sky is blue like the sea, and the grass is green like envy, and how mans sorrow is his happiness, and his joy is his pain. I can tell you the curse, and I can show you the cursed. I can explain why two plus two is four, and why four makes us all different. Trust that I would never speak blasphemy, but I can explain why their were twelve men that traveled with Jesus Christ, rather than eleven. The sun shines above us and sustains life, I explain whether that is science, or religion. I can build with all people, because all people are special, me I am just average, but I can tell you the meaning of all things if you would only listen.

———— •❖• ————

Red is like life we all desire it. Blue is like perfection we all seek it. Yellow is like trust we all need it. Orange is like money we all hunger for it. Maroon is like history we are all imprisoned by it. Black is like failure we are all subject to it. White is like power it has passed the test of time. Colors guide us all, the destination they lead us to defines them. Let the Worlds beautiful colors paint a magnificent portrait of your life, of your destiny.

———— •❖• ————

I'm on a pace for forever, like a night without a day, a day without a night. I see forever when I see you, truly touched by an angel, modeled by the hands of God, as precious as a jewel, as beautiful as the stars in the sky. I'm on a pace for forever.

———— •❖• ————

I'm on a pace for forever, where each day is one step closer to my beginning, and one step further from my ending. Like a perfect picture God has developed me, and my destiny is the portrait of perfection. Leaving it all in my hands, God has given me hope of victory, with no chance of defeat.

———————————— •❦• ————————————

I'm on a pace for forever, like the stars in the sky, my soul shines bright. I cherish the day, and give thanks for the night. In time I will know all things that have escaped my knowledge. I am forever hopeful to see tomorrow, because my Father has blessed me with sight. My teachers have been my enemies, and my students have been my friends. Together we are the same like birds of prey. We both prey on the weak, the difference is my prey gains strength to continue through life, and their prey gives strength to continue through life. Forever is like a mystery that can never be solved, torture to the ones who can not find peace, or love, a blessing to the one who prays from the day, to the night. I'm on a pace for forever, where everyday is like a mystery that can never be solved. The gift however is, everyday is like a mystery that can never be solved.

———————————— •❦• ————————————

I'm on a pace for forever where every moment is like a breath of new life, and everyday is a blessing from God. I'm on a pace for forever where each moment is but a drop in the sea of time, and everyday is like a new beginning with Christ Jesus. I'm on a pace for forever in search of new beginnings, leaving the end behind, with nothing ahead but hope for the future. I'm on a pace for forever, with each prayer giving me strength to carry on, and faith to guide me through the life, through the death, to eternity and beyond. I'm on a pace for forever, so that I can live eternal with my Father God, and Christ Jesus forever and ever. A beautiful painting, painted before the beginning, and after the end, with brushes of love, a canvas of peace, colors of joy, and happiness, with visions of now, then, and all that will be.

———————————— •❦• ————————————

The imitation of life is life itself. Life is all existence; through the teachings of Christ we learn that there is nothing but life. Death is the Devils hope. An imitation is like perfect imperfection, simple complexity, a blessed curse, blissful ignorance, good evil. An imitation of all that is an idea with no thought, a creation with no creator, an impossible possibility, life itself. It is the greatest question, with no answer, the greatest answer, with no question, life itself. Life is eternally never ending, everlasting, joyful, and full of pain, Heaven and Hell; to understand the imitation of life would be like understanding life itself. Life is like all things, its imitation would be like all things, life itself, existing with understanding, never to be understood.

Old Earth, please speak to me, I would hope to employ your wisdom in hope of a better day for myself, my family, and my friends! It is you whom holds all the knowledge of histories past, present, and future. It is you whom has eternal life under the stars, with in the cosmos that we live in. Through your eyes nothing can be hidden, no truth untold. Old Earth, I walk in honor of your magnificence each and every day, humbled by your very existence. It is you that harbors us from the great unknown that is the universe, you are our protector, you are our shelter from the storm. You are the King, for you are his Kingdom. Old Earth you have promised to house all of Gods children through all of time, and for that we are forever thankful. So I ask you, please speak to me Old Earth, I promise to give freely of all that is given, in hope of a better day.

Success always comes in the morning, defeat is left in the past, and we have life today. Tomorrow all will be forgotten, but all will remain, because we have life today, and success comes in the morning, leaving defeat in the past. If you have no fear then you are fearless, but if you have no fear then you are like fear to the fearful. Success comes in the mourning. If you look backwards it is said you will dissolve like salt, but if you follow the path of the Lord all directions lead to the Father.

Success comes in the morning in the past your defeat lives, but in the future your hope awaits. Now we have life, different from living, more like imprisonment by our Fathers love, less like existing for his holy name. A fighter will plan their peaceful resolution. A peaceful solution is only peaceful if there is a friend, anything else would be like Heaven and Hell. A friend is a man whom plans a peaceful solution, and a woman who fights for it. Life is today, leave defeat in the past, because success always comes in the mourning. If you look a man in the eye they will deceive you, what you will see is what you are shown, rather than the truth you seek. Man is only a reflection without the truth that lives inside. Today is like the truth inside of man, a seed that blossoms into the success that comes in the morning.

VI.

Science and Religion struggle to find common ground, like two parts of the same whole, like strangers in the night, like a fatherless child, like the sun to the moon, like the night to the day, like a slave to his master, like an enemy to his enemy, like Cain to Abel, like Jesus to Judas, like God to Allah, like the truth to the lie, like the wind to the sea, the mind to the body, to the soul, like the lion to the gazelle, like a bird to its prey, like the past, to the present, to the future, like struggle with no progress, like progress with no struggle. Science and religion struggle to find common ground.

The mind is scientific it analyzes, probes, and dissects. The body is metaphysical it is here, there, and nowhere. The soul is absolute it is seen, felt, and understood. The spirit is religious it is lost, found, and born again. The World is realistic it exists only as a result of our existence. The life is incomplete it is eternal, everlasting, never ending, and forever hopeful.

Conquer the World by using simple mathematics, subtract the negative, and add the positive.

Math is simple, there is a problem and an answer. Life is hard there is a problem, but not always an answer. Blessed we are to have faith to keep us strong, and hope to guide us from day to day. With out these things our math would not always add up, a problem with no answer is a problem itself. God knew this to be true so he gave us his only begotten son, to give us hope, and faith, that our problems may not always have answers, but they would always be solved.

———————— •●• ————————

The universe is a metaphor for the potential of man, woman, and child. When you see the beauty of the World know that the same beauty lives with in the heart, mind, body, and soul, of every man, woman, and child.

———————— •●• ————————

The science of psychology is religion.

———————— •●• ————————

There are only two paths in life, a negative path, and a positive path. The path to enlightenment can be achieved through both paths however; there is truth to be learned through each direction. The mathematics of the two equals to absolute zero, while the religion of the two equals to attraction, which shows Gods love for us all. The negative World attracted the son of God, and gave birth to hope through both paths, and through mathematics we see a negative World, and a positive Christ, equal to absolute joy, absolute love, absolute faith, absolute life.

———————— •●• ————————

All things consist of three geometric shapes. There is the circle, the square, and the triangle. All things created by God consist of the circle, the square, and the triangle. The circle represents life. The square represents shelter. The triangle represents intelligence. Together they represent all things past, present, and future. The circle is never ending. The square shelters us in the storm. The triangle is future peace and love. God is the creator of all things that were, that are, and that will be. It is as simple as 1, 2, 3 with our Father God. His perfect plan lives with in the circle, square, and triangle that we are all perfectly imperfect, ingenious genius, simply beautiful.

———————————— •●• ————————————

The mathematics of math is a problem, and an answer. The mathematics of life, is a problem, and a prayer. The mathematics of family, is a mother, and a father. The mathematics of victory, is defeat. The mathematics of success, is truth. The mathematics of the future, is the past, and the present. The mathematics of the World, is the people. The mathematics of science, is religion. The mathematics of power, is control. The mathematics of absolute power, is corrupt. The mathematics of evil, is hate. The mathematics of goodness, is genius. The mathematics of Jesus, is peace. The mathematics of God, is love. It is mathematics that will always let us know, what it is.

———————————— •●• ————————————

Mathematical equations are the same as biological examinations, which are the same as psychological evaluations, which are the same as scientific explanations, which are the same as sociological evolutions, which are the same as philosophical contemplations, which are the same as political elections, which are the same as that which is the same, which is one being the other.

———————————— •●• ————————————

Science is the study of natural occurrences. Natural occurrences occur due to natures existence. Nature exists as a result of Genesis. Genesis is taught in the Bible. The Bible was written by man. All glory be to God, thus God wrote the Bible. To understand Genesis is to understand scientific origins. With out Genesis science has no beginning. With no beginning there is no existence, thusly science is the study of God. The study of God is religion. Truth is, there is only religion; science is simply the study of natural occurrences.

———————————— •●• ————————————

Math is logical, science is responsible, religion is possible. Possibilities should be logical and responsible. Religion, math, and science, logical, responsible, possibilities.

———————————— •❦• ————————————

Science teaches us that everything started as a single cell organism. Religion teaches us that everything was created by God. Science teaches us that the World revolves around an axis. Religion teaches us that the World revolves around Christ. Science teaches us that we die, and our energy remains. Religion teaches us that we never truly die; we only leave Earth, to live eternally in Heaven above. Science teaches us that all things have logical explanations. Religion teaches us to walk by faith rather than sight. Science teaches us that all things evolve with time. Religion teaches us that all things have a season, and the Lord walks with us every step of the way, carrying us when we can not carry ourselves.

———————————— •❦• ————————————

Math is a perfect science, but science is imperfect, that it self is perfection. Gods perfect plan for your life is imperfection, with Jesus as your path to perfection, back to him whom created you perfectly, forever giving you hope.

———————————— •❦• ————————————

An equation for the success is peace and love, this I know because the Bible tells me so. An equation for failure is me without you, this I know because the Bible tells me so. The greatest philosophy known to man, woman, and child is peace and love, this I know because the Bible tells me so. We will all forever grow, as we grow we will inevitably know, this I know because the Bible tells me so.

———————————— •❦• ————————————

In the beginning their were two. Two became one. One became many. Now we are many, because in the beginning their were two who came together to create one. Together we are as one, apart we are two. The mathematics of the equation is one is greater than two.

Three is one step away from two, two steps away from one. At Calvary their were three bonded by one, one King, two criminals, one love. In the sky there is one sun, one moon, and millions of stars that shine bright for one World. One sun, one moon, and millions of stars shine bright for three reasons, man, woman, and child.

Jesus Christ had twelve disciples, twelve loyal followers and believers in his teachings. The twelve represent the World, and with Jesus they were thirteen, and could not be divided. Jesus however never new peace while on Earth, only war, and all that he called friend were absent in his final hour. The son of God died hanging between criminals. In his final hour Jesus only knew one friend that being him who led him to his destiny, him who hated his holy name, him who was his antithesis, the Devil. Truth is, while on Earth it was the Devil who told Christ the truth that he was the enemy of man. Gods truth lives with in that idea that the Son of Man, his only begotten son, whom he sent to the World to save from itself, never knew truth from any he called friend, only from him who wished to destroy him, the Devil.

VII.

Great minds think alike, but great minds do not think alike, that would be crazy.

––––––––––– •◦• –––––––––––

Whoever said "School is for fools" must be a fool them self. School is nothing more than a metaphor, a preparation for life and for death. The lessons learned guide us through life, death, and beyond; and as we matriculate our commencement will be awaiting us in Heaven above.

––––––––––– •◦• –––––––––––

In school there is remedial, honors, and advance. Pepper, Salt and Pepper, Salt. Poverty, middle-class, wealthy. Logically speaking ignorant, intelligent, genius. Time has revealed pepper to be the salt of genius. God is truly good.

––––––––––– •◦• –––––––––––

In nature all things are like a metaphor for life that is a great vision of knowledge, and truth for some, but all can not see the truth. Those whom can not see the truth should not worry however, them who can are also blind to what is true. It is God whom has written all that is truth, and who sees all that is hidden from the eyes of man. It is Man who must seek the truth and discover who he is, and guide everyone through the darkness, to the light.

———— •❦• ————

A metaphor is something that represents something else, like a peaceful day, or a calm breeze, or a bright sky. The nature of life is metaphorical. Man is a metaphor himself, for what, depends on the man. In life we see through our eyes, but understand through our heart, mind, and soul. Our pain can sometimes cloud our vision, our past can sometimes haunt our future, and our choices can sometimes lead us away from our purpose. Those are examples of life metaphors, they represent life situations. There is another metaphor however that is metaphor itself, and represents all others, that is Father God. God is the creator of all things seen, and unseen, known, and yet to be known. God is truly the greatest metaphor of all, because his holy name represents all things.

———— •❦• ————

A simile is the comparison of two unlike things, typically using like or as. Like a good father. Like an obedient son. Like a loving mother. Like a caring daughter. Like the break of dawn. Like the king of the jungle. Like Heaven above. Like Hell on Earth. Like a beautiful day. Like a dark night. Like a lonely soul. Like abundant joy. Like a bird in flight. Like tears of a clown. Like perfect harmony. Like the beat of the drum. Like the beat of the heart. Like the soundtrack to life. Like a fearless warrior. Like a decorated soldier. Like a passionate leader. Like me, and you. Like today. Like tomorrow. Like yesterday. Like forever. Like the end. Like the beginning. That is simile, as life with no God, with no hope, with no Christ, truly incomplete.

———— •❦• ————

It is ironic that your friend can be your enemy. It is ironic that you live to die. It is ironic that the truth is a secret, and the lie is known. It is ironic that you live in man, but are born in woman. It is ironic that the grass is green, and the sun is yellow, and the sky is blue. It is ironic that war can bring peace and love. It is ironic that the World continuously revolves, but man can stand still. It is ironic that we love and hate with our heart. It is ironic that we see with our eyes, hear with our ears, but

84

understand with our heart. It is ironic that God, Jesus, and the Holy Spirit are one, but the World is divided. The World is chaotic, and it is ironic that irony can bring clarity to the chaos.

———————————•●•———————————

When you dream you are asleep, but when you awaken your dream has ended; the irony is, your dream ends when it begins. When you cry, tears come down from your eyes; the irony is, your eyes feel no pain. When you are faced with an obstacle you have three choices, go around it, go through it, or turn back; the irony is, all three defeat the obstacle, if it is destined it will be. When you look to the sky you can see many colors; the irony is, you can not touch any of them, you can only see them. When you travel long distances you will naturally get tired; the irony is, when you get tired you have naturally traveled long distances. When you fight your enemy somebody will lose; the irony is, when you give your enemy peace no one loses. When you study you will naturally learn; the irony is, that when you learn you must naturally teach. When you lose something it may never be found; the irony is, when you find something it is no longer lost. When you stop you must eventually go; the irony is, when you have stopped you can never go. When there is a light at the end of the tunnel you will always have hope; the irony is, that when there is no light at the end of the tunnel you will always have hope. The irony always is, is. That is ironic.

———————————•●•———————————

The true nature of business is money rather than people. A business grows from the money that is earned rather than as a result of any good done for the people. I choose to redefine the nature of business however, investing my time in understanding, the understanding of people. I grow as a result of every positive relationship gained, so you can never say I am not about my business that would be untrue.

———————————•●•———————————

Every action has an equal or positive reaction. Every reaction has a consequence. Every consequence has an effect on our lives. A choice of positive actions will always benefit positive reactions, affecting your life equally, as positive, with no consequence.

———————— •❦• ————————

A fact is something that has been proven to be true, thus making everyone like facts to the ones they love, because we all have proven to be true, to the ones we love; and our very existence, our very being, is proof that God is real, and he is love, there is no truer fact.

———————— •❦• ————————

Alpha and omega are the beginning and the end. A wise scholar once wrote, "The omega is the alpha, and the alpha is the omega, like a warriors birth is the end of war, or like betrayal is sight to the blind. Omega is alpha since in the end their has to be a new beginning, whether it is a new existence of nothing, or new existence of something new. The beginning is omega, and the ending is alpha, because alpha ends what is hindering a new beginning.".

———————— •❦• ————————

Where we are is in between the beginning and the end, some where between here and now. We are presently in the present headed towards the future leaving the past behind. We live on planet Earth, floating amongst the stars, some where hidden with in space and time. Our position is fixed with in infinity and eternity, like time we are continuously moving, from where we are, to where we will be; where we will end, only time will tell. Our reality exists in our existence, our existence however exists where we are, some where between the beginning and the end, floating amongst the stars, hidden with in space and time, here and now, the past, present, future, and beyond.

———————— •❦• ————————

At the center there is peace. A centered mind is king. To be centered is to have balance. A centered body is strong and able. In nature all things are centered, with man however, the center is a purposeful search that can last a life time. Man must search to be centered like birds search for prey, like the night searches for day, like woman searches for man, like death searches for life, like the beginning searches for the ending. A mans search for the center is a purposeful search for peace and love, wisdom, balance, and strength. Some search their entire life and never succeed, till one day they realize they have been their the whole time, while others search through eternity, and a day, and never find that which makes them centered, that which makes them whole, that which defines them. Truth is, the center is a search for nothing, what you will find once it is found is nothing that you have not always possessed.

------------------------•●•------------------------

Today we stand at the center of victory and defeat, tragedy and triumph, hope and despair. No one truly knows what tomorrow will bring, right now our fate depends on our next decision, our next move; which move will you make, which path will you take. Like a game of Chess every move is important, and dependent on every move, leading you to your victory, or your inevitable defeat. The choice you make can lead you to your destiny of destiny or your fate of fate. Choose wisely, because the choice you make today, can determine the life you have tomorrow.

------------------------•●•------------------------

Law or lawless? Young or old? Me or you? Us or them? Together or apart? Up or down? Light or dark? Rich or poor? Weak or strong? Faith or fear? Knowledge or power? Fact or fiction? Science or religion? Friend or foe? What will be?

------------------------•●•------------------------

In the end their will be nothing. We began as nothing, and were made to something. We began as nothing and lived as something. To go from nothing to something, back to nothing is the circle of life. In the beginning their is life. In the end their will be life. Life eternal.

———————————•●•———————————

Our life is governed by fate; we walk through life at the mercy of it. We all have absolute power over that which we do, but yet in still fate governs us. The impossibility of that idea is a question to many, and scholars and philosophers of all degrees have pondered that idea through time. They say that fate can not exist when man has free will, which is something that can be understood, but to understand God, and Jesus Christ impossibilities can become very possible. Understanding Christ, and the Father brings me to the belief that all is possible in the name of God. When I see the World, and the people, and all that is, I can never question the power of God, but the mystery of fate and free will, will forever be a mystery. I still however will forever walk through life as a man that is blind to his destiny, living my life for God, with knowledge that my fate awaits me.

———————————•●•———————————

Monday the second day of the week, where the weekend is behind us, and the week is in front of us. Where the start of something new begins, and the end of something old starts. Like an impossibility there is no turning back. Monday be like life and death past, present, and future, what awaits can only be known on Tuesday. Wait on Tuesday simply because Monday is here, and when Tuesday comes we can all say it was worth the wait, simply because Monday taught us patience, and Tuesday fulfilled our purpose. On Tuesday we can then reflect on Mondays victories. From their we can build and move forward through Wednesday, and be hopeful that on Thursday we will not be alone. When Friday comes everyone can look back on the journey, all because we waited on Tuesday, but for now we enjoy Monday.

———————————•●•———————————

There are two sides to every story, the left and the right. The difference is one side is the truth, and the other side is the lie. If two men are standing in opposition of one another, and one is on the left going right, and the other is on the right going left, they will eventually cross paths. Physics teaches us that two bodies can not occupy the same space that I believe is the true nature of peace, love, war, hate, space, time, evolution, creation, purpose, destiny, fate. Bodies that can never occupy the same space yet all exist in reality are eternally in conflict, forever searching for resolution. In the end the man who is headed the right way will be left and right, a mystery of time, religion, science, virtue, truth, lie, past, present and future. Two men, two directions, one way.

———————————— •●• ————————————

The prequel to success is failure, so truth is we are all forever hopeful. The prequel to us is you, so truth be like the both of us. The prequel to life is the parents life, so give all glory to God. The prequel to the struggle is the struggle, therefore struggle defines itself. The prequel to divorce is marriage; therefore one should marry their soul mate so you will never be divided. The prequel to the sequel is that which defines us all, and gives us all meaning in the end.

———————————— •●• ————————————

If you build something and it is destroyed, you can always rebuild it, but if you destroy something that has been built, you can never destroy it again, therefore the destroyer has been defeated; so the lost are like martyrs to the World, their loss will forever be remembered for the defeat of that which lead them astray. In the end there will be nothing left but hope for a new day.

———————————— •●• ————————————

The greatest mystery can never be solved because it is the greatest mystery. The tallest building can never fall because it is the tallest. Your best friend will never betray you because they are your best friend. The most beautiful day can never be ugly because it is most beautiful. The kindest act can never be unkind because it is the kindest. The most complicated equation can never be equated because it is most complicated. We are all imprisoned by our truth, truly no imprisonment at all, like a blessing in disguise it will set us free.

The most beautiful thing in the World would have to be positive direction, with no guilt left behind. Beauty can come in many ways, the best being the way to the Father, the way to the Kingdom, the way to salvation, the way to paradise, the way to peace and love, the way to Christ, through Christ, with Christ, Abraham, Moses, and Elijah. Beautiful is the direction that leads us home, beauty is the hope that we will never be lead astray.

Contemplations of the mind are childish preoccupations. A mans thoughts should be centered in reality. His thoughts govern his every move, his every action, his every decision. The reality that a man lives in is his truth, while his minds contemplations hold all his dreams and aspirations, only to be satisfied in reality.

There is an old saying which says, "Fight fire with fire.", that saying is intrinsically impossible, yet in still holds infinite possibility. One can never truly fight fire with more fire, one can however overcome hate with their hatred for it. To hate hatred is to love what is love. Ones love for peace can lead them on an epic war against war. Such a saying as "Fight fire with fire" seems impossible yet holds all the possibility to obtain victory, and defeat, defeat, to win, to overcome all that would hope to stand in opposition of that which is peace that which is love.

Never take a bite out of what you can not chew. Never speak before you think. Never teach before you are taught. Never spend before you have earned. Never look directly into the sun, you will go blind, only look directly to the son, so you can see. Never talk to strangers, strange things may occur. Never argue with a foolish person that would be foolish. Never trust someone who does not trust them self. Never answer a question before you ask a question. Never say never.

————————•●•————————

What greater ill is it to take food out of the mouth of a starving child? This question is a metaphor for responsibility, the responsibility we have to care for one another. Confusion is the Devils vice, and it tends to be in the midst of much we do, say, and see. It tends to lead us away from our responsibility to serve, and towards a preoccupation for self serving vices. What greater ill is it to take the food out of the mouth of a starving child? None I would suspect, it seems that that is the true nature of evil, vice itself that which has plagued us all since the fall of man in the Garden of Eden.

————————•●•————————

Ask questions and you will get answers, it is just that simple. Look first and speak second, and you will avoid what is presently tragic and escape future tragedy, it is just that simple. Life is like a circle what goes around comes around, it is just that simple. The greatest philosophical question is, where are we, it is just that simple. Simple things are the root of all things complicated, it is just that simple.

————————•●•————————

Why must the good die young and the bad live long and prosperous? The answer is simple, the lie. A wise man once said, ". . . let the lie have what it has because truth is, the truth is truly everything.". Truth is, the good never truly die young, because they are promised life everlasting through Christ, and their memory will forever live on through all that praise his holy name.

————————•●•————————

Our limit is in the sky, therefore there truly is no limit, because the sky truly is endless. The sky is a reflection of the mind, a reflection of thought, a reflection of inspiration, a reflection of reflection. Its beauty and magnificence holds all the possibility that man possesses inside. We are all limitless, there is no limit to our potential. God placed the sky high above us, not so it could be reached, but rather for it to be reached for.

———•◦•———

If you think before you act, you will never have to act; this is an actual, actualization of thought.

———•◦•———

The second you lose something someone else is sure to find something; the reason being is that when something is lost it can never be found unless it is lost, so when something is lost it is inevitable that something will be found.

———•◦•———

In the game of Chess the queen can move in every direction, while the king has but one move. The queens power is like the kings strength. Her power is like the kings love. Her power is the king himself. Having only one move the king truly has no power, however through the love of his queen the king becomes the most powerful piece of them all, that is as clear as the day itself. The king is the queen in the game of Chess, power, love, sacrifice, courage. The queen is like a woman defending her man; however it is the man whom we see through the woman's love. In Chess all the pieces move for the king, the king truly needs but one move. In the game of Chess like in life it is the kings kingdom which defines him, which holds all his truth, power, and glory.

———•◦•———

The music of life is composed by the people who live it, exist in it, and perish from its loss. The finished composition is what we hear when there is nothing to be heard. Like harmonious perfection we hear nothing but beautiful music in a World of imperfect harmony.

———————————•❖•———————————

Smooth like a jazz crooner, fast like the keys of the piano, strong like the beat of a drum, and harmonious like the trumpet of Louis Armstrong himself! Music is like armor to all whom would wish to corrupt the beat of my heart.

———————————•❖•———————————

If you listen to your heart, your heart will listen to you. If you hear beautiful music, your spirit, heart, and soul will be in beautiful harmony. When you sing from the heart, you will touch the soul. When you dance joyfully, you will walk faithfully. Music is a gift to all who are surrounded by it, and a curse to all who fail to hear the music.

———————————•❖•———————————

Music to the mind is like love to the heart, like warmth in the cold, shelter in the rain, like friendship in the land of your enemy, like salvation to the soul.

———————————•❖•———————————

The day came when the boy left home. When the day came that the boy returned home their was no home at all. The home that the boy once knew was no more; because the boy was the heart, and home is where the heart is. When the boy returned he was no longer a boy, he was a man, and his heart had turned cold, and their truly is no home for the heartless . . .

———————————•❖•———————————

A bird flew down and laid rest on the shoulders of a boy. As the sun set, and the stars began to shine, all the Worlds people moved unknowingly, as if the King had not just been born . . .

One step lead to another, and another, until the road was no more, and their was only open space, vast as the eyes could see. Their was no direction to be traveled, but long distances to go. In the end the oasis would be home, and the home would be called Earth . . .

Sun light beamed down from Heaven above awakening the sleeping beauty. The light shined upon her head illuminating the hair as fine as silk weaved by the Lord himself. She was as precious as the most precious jewel, and as beautiful as the most beautiful of days the World has known. Her existence gave definition to purpose, and meaning to life. A purposeful, meaningful life for man, and with in her womb she held the hope of the future . . . The only flaw she knew was man.

"I'd never be a slave, I'd rather be dead in my grave . . .", this is the song we sing, but our ancestors were kings and queens, stripped from their homeland, made to be slaves, cotton pickers, field hands, concubines, house servants. So we must all forever celebrate the life, and death, of every man, woman. and child who suffered; and live everyday in memoriam of our ancestors, who lived, and died, as American slaves.

Slave child I feel your pain, born into a World that is not your own, sentenced to a life of servitude, serving your enemy, hopelessly burdened by the evil that men do. Slave child I feel your pain, cursed by birth into a World were your skin shackles you for the transgressions of your enemy. Slave child I feel your pain, destined for life as a slave, a life with no meaning with no freedom. Slave child I shed tears for you, and live in memory of your life lost in servitude and pain, for the purpose of suffrage, which truly holds no purpose at all. Slave child you will never be forgotten, and will forever live in the hearts of men.

———————————•◦•———————————

Journey men travel for the purpose of the righteous path. Whether glorious or wicked the purposeful journey will always be to the glory of the righteous path. Journey men each step backwards is cowardly, therefore march courageously to the path that is yours. Know that all purpose be to the righteous path. Journey men look down when facing an obstacle and see what you truly face. In the race through the righteous and wicked path alike a journey man will never be lead astray. All purposeful distance traveled be to the journey mans glorious journey through the righteous and wicked and path alike leading them to glory!

———————————•◦•———————————

Our native sons struggle to forge an identity in this new World. They speak with no voice, no power behind their words. They are at war with themselves, their influences reflect no truth of whom they are, or what they are, they truly do not know. We are forever hopeful however through amazing grace that we will always receive a gift of guidance from a gifted guide, like an angel that guides us from Heaven above, and speaks for those whom can not speak for themselves.

———————————•◦•———————————

A man can search for the end until his dying day. The end eludes us like a squirrel in the tree, as a mouse in the field, as a pig in the sty, it is allusive! Truth is, the ending may never come. In the end there is nothing, all that was will be a memory, and all that will be will never be known. In the end there is nothing, their truly is nothing in the end. Mans search should not be for the end, but rather for a new beginning. One should redefine their quest for the end, and simply search for what is "over". When something is over there is a new beginning, one can rebuild like King Jesus of Nazareth the carpenter and start a new beginning, knowing that your search is "over", but that it is not the end.

The hope of man is inside woman. A woman is the secret of war like the defeat of Goliath by David, and the fall of Sodom and Gomorrah. Inside a woman our savior was born, and inside the World our savior died, and inside a woman our savior will be born again. A woman is destined to bring peace and love to the World, destined to carry man through eternity. The hope of the World will come from a woman, and defeat all that has kept man from a woman's love. Like a king in his kingdom the womb of a woman holds eternal hope, and the hope that is within holds us all.

The meaning of life is the law, live by it and nothing can keep you from your dreams; those who choose not to will see all their dreams slowly fade away like the clouds in the sky. The law that governs us is that which protects us. We all collectively create the law, but God has created us. All that we deem law has been given to us by the Father, to use, learn, protect, and helps us evolve as people, where we all are justifiably guided to our rightful place in space, and time. The deeper understanding is with in the universe we live; but the law as known by man is our meaning that defines us, and guides us through life, with the hope that we will all have that which God has given to us.

The true nature of the law is to protect the innocent from the guilty; the truth from the lie; so if you have a dream live by the laws of the land, and nothing will keep you from its fulfillment.

A man of the law has little power against another man of the law. In life there are times when the law must be held up against the law, because what is designed for good does not always have good outcomes. A criminal is easy prey for a man of the law, while a man who lives by the law presents his innocence with no guilt. Man is the law, but man is inherently guilty. Every person is born in to sin; therefore we must all strive to be men of the law, in order to live freely. There truly is only one true judge, and until the day comes that we meet him, we all must build castles of innocence, with no walls of guilt, because no man can truly judge another; so the law protects us from one another, because we are all truly guilty until proven innocent.

Innocence and guilt are one in the same. There are no innocent with out the guilty, and there is no guilty with out the innocent. Two parts of the same whole can never truly be divided. It is the blood that makes us one; therefore Christ has truly never left the World, he lives forever in Heaven, and inside each man, woman, and child. It is true we are centered through Christ and can never truly be divided, whether guilty or innocent, we are all forever hopeful for salvation.

There are no man made words, all knowledge comes from above, thus all words are given to us by the Father. Words become language, and the language becomes the law that governs us. Respect the law. The words that we use have a way of defining who we are, choose your words carefully, because they can be used against you in a court of law. A word is nothing but a thought, translated into a meaning that motivates an action, which can lead one into serious trouble, with serious consequences. This contemplation on words and law is just one of many, but I gather the most important, because this is a contemplation on the power of words to govern, and keep us free; free so that our words become art rather than law.

In the Bible we learn the "Art of Man". We see the power of God. We understand the struggle of kings. We are educated by wise words. We are intrigued by mystery, and suspense. We are taught right from wrong. We are taught the power of prayer. We marvel at the scriptures of Jesus Christ. We feel the pain of the people. We understand the love of Christ, through his life, death, and resurrection. We see the past, present, and future through the pages of the Bible. We are instructed to honor thy mother and thy father, and to love thy neighbor as you love thyself. We see, understand, are educated, intrigued, taught, marvel, feel, know, view, and are instructed in the ways of the World, in order to live life, through eternity, and beyond.

—•—

The seven deadly sins, lust, gluttony, greed, sloth, wrath, envy, and pride all represent a vice that can lead to death, literally, and figuratively. Lust can lead one to desire that which is undesirable. Gluttony can lead one to indulge in indulgence. Greed can lead one to want material wealth, rather than spiritual wealth. Sloth can lead one to walk when they should run. Wrath can lead one to self destruct from with in like a cancer. Envy can lead one to lose sight of what is and see what is not. Pride is the most deadly of the seven deadly sins, pride can lead one to see God as them self, and them self as God.

—•—

The true nature of evil is circular, it has no known beginning, nor ending that is like power, seemingly impossible to defeat, or understand. Evil however, is not power, rather that which defines the powerful. Evil is circular, it starts with a question, and ends with a question; you start with a battle and end with a war. Hope however is that their is nothing impossible in the name of God. To defeat evil God gave his only son to the World to be the center of all things. Christ the King, the most powerful defined by his power to defeat evil. One must be centered through Christ and discover their truth, and defeat the evil that binds them. End the cycle of hate that can surround you, your family, and all that you love.

— •◉• —

Biblical scholars though time have pondered the question of why Judas Iscariot committed suicide. Some suggest that his guilt over came him and lead him to take his own life. Others suggest the Devil some how influenced him to hang himself from a tree. The answer can never truly be known. A wise scholar once stated, "Judas Iscariot never truly committed suicide."; they suggest that his death was a metaphor for his loss, as Christ was ". . . life itself." his betrayal was his true death, and that his suicide took his body, but his betrayal of Christ took his hope, heart, soul, love, friend, and blessed life.

— •◉• —

The Bible teaches us "The last shall be first and the first shall be last.". This teaches us that the first is somehow wrong, and the last is somehow right. I suggest that that it is not necessarily true that the first is somehow wrong, and that the last is somehow right. Instead I see that idea as a circular philosopher would, and understand it to mean that the last, and the first, will somehow be as one in the end.

— •◉• —

If you fall victim to circumstance that does not mean your circumstances make you a victim. The teachings of the Good Book teach us that man has a friend in Jesus, so let your circumstances strengthen you, rather than define you. With Jesus as a friend, you can never truly be alone, and will forever be hopeful for paradise, truly a gift from God. A gift from God is like Christmas everyday. Truth is, to open Gods gift is like opening your eyes for the first time, though you have never been blind.

— •◉• —

Faith is strength in the storm. Search for happiness, live for love, die for peace find your purpose, and pursue it purposefully. Give even when not given to. Look for the good in people rather than the bad, the strength inside, rather than the outer weakness. That is virtue, blessings that bring you to the Father; we are all prodigal at birth, our Fathers only hope is that one day we will find our way back home.

I am faithful, so the truth lives in me, my brothers, and my sisters that I truly believe. The World however as seen by a wise philosopher, ". . . holds no truth.", ". . . the truth is, there is no truth." The truth is hidden from the World to forever remain secret, everything that is left is the lie. The lie is like a mystery that can never be solved because it holds no truth. "We truly live in Hell". The wise philosopher however teaches us that "Jesus is our savior and our King, because through his grace we are covered from the flames of Hell, and through his love all our thirsts are quenched.".

VIII.

No man seeks betrayal, so no man should wish to be called betrayer.

————— •●• —————

Your enemies eyes hold no truth beloved children of God; they see you for not who you are, how God has made you, but rather for how they would wish you to be. They see you in a distorted reflection of their hatred for you, their hatred for themselves. Your enemies eyes hold no truth; so it would not serve you to engage in debate or any form of dispute with them who are against you, for the purpose of truth. Sad it may be that would be like an impossible possibility. Let them be as they are, alone, and pray for them, in hope that one day they will see.

————— •●• —————

Sometimes the greatest punishment is to give a man just what they desire. Let them who desire the World, live in it.

————— •●• —————

Your enemies fatal flaw is their name . . . , the World we live in as children of God is built on truth, therefore one should be the truth. Defeat all foes by living the truth, for what greater ill is it to be the enemy of the truth, in a World were truth is law.

————— •●• —————

Your enemies ignorance is your bliss. What they are ignorant of is the very reason they are that they are, and you are whom you are. Their ignorance holds no truth except that it is ignorance. Their ignorance is the answer to why there is conflict between you. It is blissful like the absence of power in defeat. They have no power against your victory, or your defeat; because their ignorance holds no truth, it only answers the question as to why they are that they are, and you are whom you are.

––––––•●•––––––

The nature of a spy is to become their enemies friend so that they can defeat them from with in, like a cancer. That is a method of war; it is also a method of peace. A peaceful man also befriends their enemy in order to defeat them, the only difference however is, through peace the enemy is cured of the cancer with truth, and through war the enemy is succumbed by the cancer, with the lie that will inevitably destroy them.

––––––•●•––––––

A story is never complete until it is finished, and a story can never be finished until it is complete; therefore the story teller is truly king. The end can only come from him whom tells the story.

––––––•●•––––––

Tragedy will strike the righteous and wicked alike, the difference is one is innocent, and the other is guilty. The guilty walk to tragedy into defeat, and the innocent walk through tragedy into their victory.

––––––•●•––––––

My enemy is a genius but they can never defeat me because I choose peace and love rather than war and hate. That is victory for peace and love, and defeat for war and hate.

––––––•●•––––––

Do not wait on strangers, wait on your friends. Do not argue with fools, build with intellectuals. Do not sweat the little things, work out the big things. Do not leave anything behind, take everything with you. Do not fight your enemy, give them peace.

———————————————— •●• ————————————————

God requires that one learn from their enemy, the reason being is there is nothing more humbling then to be taught by the one who wishes to destroy you. The lessons learned however are no curse, rather blessings, because no truth learned can lead one away from their destiny, it will only lead them to it. Once you have arrived, and have fulfilled your destiny, the lessons learned will be knowledge, power, wisdom, virtue, and servitude, humbled by the one who wished to destroy you.

IX.

One truth can defeat every lie . . .

--- •●• ---

Searching for the truth is pointless. The point is the truth searches for you. The search begins at birth and ends at birth. That is the point.

--- •●• ---

The only thing that is forever is truth. The truth lives on from generation to generation, while the lie withers and fades away like dust in the wind. Truth stands the test of time, like the words of a master poet the truth is embedded in our mind, soul, and body. It is truth that defines us, while that which is the lie hides whom we truly are. The truth is in all that we see, for what lie can be seen through the eyes of man. What is truth is a simple question that governs us, inspires us, and defines all that we are. There is no denying the truth that is in nature, for nature holds the truth like a mother to their new born child. There is nothing forever but truth. The truth is a promise, a gift of hope, that their always will be a new day.

--- •●• ---

All there is, is truth, everything else is a lie.

--- •●• ---

The true nature of truth is forever. Their is no death for that which is true, it protects us against the lie, it is our armor against evil. There is no greater evil than the lie. That which is a lie leads us down the path of wickedness, while that which is truth leads us to our every hearts desire. The truth lives eternally through our children's, children, children, the lie simply fades away like dust in the wind. The true nature of truth is forever, everlasting, it was before the beginning, and will be after the end.

———————•●•———————

The lie runs from its destiny, while the truth searches for that which is destined. At the center there is a great battle, the lie that has been truth, or the truth that will be destined.

———————•●•———————

Search for truth like the night searches for the day, like the heart searches for the heartless, like the mind searches for clarity, like man searches for knowledge, like the beginning searches for the end, like death searches for life, like life searches for eternity, as woman searches for man, like pain searches for joy, like peace searches for love. Search for truth like your life depends on it, because what is life with out knowledge of self but an endless journey with no beginning, nor end.

———————•●•———————

A lie can never destroy the truth; it can only hide what is true.

———————•●•———————

If the truth will set you free, then the lie will imprison you. If light hides the darkness, then darkness must hide the light. If man can rule the World, then the World can also rule man. If Mother Nature is a woman, and Father Time is a man, then the Four Seasons must be their children. If the sun sets in the west, and rises in the east, then the World must be the center. If we are all children of God, then the only thing that separates us must be our faith. If you never knew a friend, but also never knew an enemy, then you must be king.

Humble me with the truth, rather than subduing me with the lie.

The truth about truth is there is no lie. The truth about today is tomorrow. The truth about the heart is the soul. The truth about me is you. The truth about forever is the end. The truth about life is death. The truth about peace is love.

The truth should never fear the lie because the lie is the truth. Life should never fear death because death is life. The past should never fear the future because the future is the past. The day should never fear the night because the night is the day. Love should never fear hate because hate is love. Sadness should never fear happiness because happiness is sadness. A friend should never fear an enemy because an enemy is a friend. Man should never fear, fear because fear is man.

One Lie can imprison you, but one truth will set you free . . .

If truth be told what would come would be like an avalanche from a mountain so high it would reach the clouds, and eclipse the sky. If truth be told what would come would be like a solar shower of many moons, and millions of stars. If truth be told what would come would be like the greatest discovery known to man, the truth! If truth be told what would come would change space and time, the past and present, and create a new future. If truth be told what would come? Would you? I know I certainly would, truth be told.

———•●•———

The only thing that can defeat the lie is truth; therefore the truth is truly undefeatable.

———•●•———

The lie is like knowledge of something untrue, truly knowledge of nothing. The night is like the days mask, it hides the face of the light. The day is like the hope of the slave, freedom from the darkness. Destiny is like a mathematical equation, there is only result. Religion is like physics, when you send your prayers up blessings come down. Trust is like faith, when someone gives it to you, you only have it if you believe. Peace is like love we only have it if we are as one.

———•●•———

A real lie is like a fake truth, truly the lie.

———•●•———

Truth be like a star in the sky that does not shine, it is their but you must search for it. Truth be like a story that begins but never ends, truly everlasting, like a defeated warrior, eternally peaceful, similar to obsession, determined to be, clearly the answer with no question, like a solution with no problem. Truth be like both, because both is always true, but there is only one truth, truly amazing, like a World that exist in space and time, lost but forever found. Truth be like your name, so we are all forever hopeful to be truth.

———•●•———

Nothing that is told will ever matter if no one believes you.

———•●•———

What is secret can never be known. What is known can never be secret. What is truth can never be a lie. What is a lie can never be truth. What is fated can never be denied. What is denied can never be fated. What is love can never be hate. What is hate can never be love. What is given by the Lord can never be taken. What is taken can never have been given by the Lord.

———————————•●•———————————

A definition is only a definition if it is defined by truth, any other definition would definitely be a lie.

———————————•●•———————————

A secret is something that can never be known. A secret can be told, and still never be known, because it is secret. A secret is like mystery that can never be solved. To solve the mystery would be revealing what is secret, like a secret that is known. What is a secret but something that exists with no existence, something that is here but not there, something that is perceived but not seen, something that is taught, but can never be learned, a word with a definition, but no meaning.

———————————•●•———————————

A mystery of truth is no mystery at all, because the truth is known, the lie is what is secret.

———————————•●•———————————

The only thing I fear is the fact. The fact is like truth, but more like the vice of the lie. A fact can be the death of the truth. It can be the Devils plan manifested. It can be a lie disguised as truth. It can destroy life. It can redefine what is good. It can turn innocence to guilt, and the guilty into the innocent. It can turn man against man, and leave children lost in a lonely World. It can lead to war, and defeat peace. It can taint the pure, and poison the well. I only fear the fact that can turn what is truth, into what is a lie, and what is a lie into what is truth. That is a fact.

———————————•●•———————————

Every action has an equal or positive reaction that is the first law of physics. The first law of physics is like truth, because there is only truth, negatively or positively. Every circle has an ending and a beginning, the truth about both however is only known by the creator of the circle. Every square has four corners, but every square is not the same, like every man has a heart, but all men do not have heart.

———————————•●•———————————

Truth is both science and religion. Both fact and fiction. Both reality and fantasy. Both past, present, and future. Both the ending and the beginning. Both here and there. Both love and hate. Both me and you. Both friend and foe. Both Heaven and Hell. Both life and death. Both man, woman, and child. Both night and day. Both yes and no. Both pain and joy. Both rich and poor. Both master and slave. Both king, queen, and kingdom. Both peace and love. Truth is both, truly amazing, truly everything.

———————————•●•———————————

If you want to know the truth ask that which is true. If you wish to know the lie tell the truth, and them who oppose you will be your answer.

———————————•●•———————————

Be the truth and defeat them that are your lie.

———————————•●•———————————

The truth is like seeing something for the first time that you have already seen millions of times, finally understanding its meaning, its significance, its truth, and truly knowing what you see. Truth, the man behind the mask.

———————————•●•———————————

Every story has two sides, the truth and the lie.

———— •●• ————

The truth about the World is that the World holds no truth. The truth about truth is that the truth is the World.

———— •●• ————

A war for the purpose of peace is spiritual, while war for the purpose of war is that which it is.

———— •●• ————

The truth can never destroy itself, and the lie has no true power over that which is true, therefore the truth is the greatest weapon of all.

———— •●• ————

The Devil does not know the truth, he only knows the truth.

———— •●• ————

The lie will deny the existence of the truth, yet in still say it is the truth itself. I know this to be true because of histories past, presents future, futures defeat, friends, enemies, corrupt leaders, lost sons, impoverished teachers, wealthy criminals, evil genius, casualties of war, war before peace, love before hate, a kiss before betrayal, Christ's crucifixion, God and the Devil.

———— •●• ————

The Devil is the greatest warrior, his fatal flaw however is that his enemy is the truth, and the lie can never defeat the truth that would be a lie.

———— •●• ————

To know something is to have absolute power over truth. Absolute truth be like you and me. Together we are truth; apart we are the lie, truly the Devils vice.

———— •●• ————

Truth is their can only be one truth but many lies, and we are all truly guilty as sin. Our only hope for innocence is the Lords forgiveness.

———— •●• ————

Truth is like deaths reincarnation, life eternal.

———— •●• ————

There is an old saying which says, "What goes up must come down." which is very true. The truth however is that "What goes up must come down", but also what goes down must come up.

———— •●• ————

The Lords gift is the same for everyone and everything; he only gives us truth.

———— •●• ————

The truest revelation of a man is that they are a man.

———— •●• ————

In time all truth will be known, and all lies will have been made truth; place your faith in the Lord, and in time you will be.

———— •●• ————

Truth is, the birth of Jesus Christ is the secret of war. Truth is, war is sin manifested and personified by the evil that men do. Truth is, Jesus was sent to us to defeat sin peacefully. Truth is, Jesus did the impossible by dying by the hands of sinful men. Truth is, his death defeated sin by giving man new hope through his life, death, and resurrection. Truth is, there is still war and sin, but through Jesus' death and resurrection we all have hope for forgiveness, and eternal life in Heaven above. Truth is, that is the way Jesus defeated sin peacefully. Truth is, King Jesus Christ of Nazareth the Messiah is truth, and truth is the secret of war.

Epilogue

In the end there is always a new beginning. Our beginning is as a result of our purposeful journey through the pages of this book. I celebrate our newly formed collective conscious, and pray that truth, understanding, and a renewed faith has been achieved. With in the pages of this collection of thoughts and ideas, I hope that any whom have been a witness to what lies with in have been inspired in someway, form, or fashion to live, and with life as your purpose we will all be victorious, this I know because the Bible tells me so. I hope that all whom have journeyed through the pages of *Peace & Love* smiled, laughed, cried, contemplated truth, and lie, were intrigued by something new, or something old made anew, I hope that the time spent was time that added to the betterment of all whom explored what was inside the pages of this book. The truth can never truly be told from any man, woman, or child; as human beings, children of God, we are all at the mercy of our own ignorance, and are forever at odds with our own guilt. In the end our hope lies with in yesterdays yet to come, with in tomorrows mystery, with in past failures and successes, with in our gift of life, and our promise of eternity. As we live and grow, and travel through space and time, so will we become that much closer to what is truth. I hope that with in the pages of *Peace & Love* I have been able to contribute, to what degree I know not, a piece of honest, sincere ideology, reflecting a human perspective with nothing but truth as my verdict. In the end I believe that until the day we walk through the pearly gates in Heaven above, and are judged before our Father God, our answer must always be peace and love, this I believe is a purposeful quest with no possibility of failure. To fail would be no failure at all, because a search for peace and love can never lead one astray, it is the absence of it that will inevitably lead us all on path of destruction, which is the Devils hope, rather than a path to eternity, which is Gods promise. Let truth be told and we will forever have peace and love!

About the Author

Leland Bedford is from Louisville, Ky., and was born in Houston, TX., he and his family relocated from Texas when Leland was still a baby. His childhood home was located in a suburb located just outside the Louisville city limits, and he enjoyed a happy upbringing with himself, his older sister, and his parents. Upon completion of high school he applied, and was accepted to Morehouse College in Atlanta, Ga. where he majored in English literature. While attending Morehouse Leland enjoyed the freedom of being away from home and excelled in the beginning of his college matriculation, however as he matriculated through college he began to fall victim to the pitfalls of big city life and being away from home. His troubles lead him down many different paths, which extended his matriculation and caused him much mental, physical, emotional, and economical hardship. Through it all however, Leland continued to pursue a B.A. in English literature from Morehouse, and received his degree in 2005. Upon completion of college he entered the work field full-time and worked while mending all his wounds from his time in college. After graduating from Morehouse he relocated back to Louisville, Ky where he currently lives. His time in college helped strengthen him as a man, and gave him love for the written word, and knowledge as a whole. It was in college that he found deep interest in self, and thusly all that helps define him as a man. His time at Morehouse was very beneficial and enjoyable, and left him with a seed to water, and grow, into something that would hopefully add to the greater good of humanity. *Peace & Love* is his first published book, and is a child of his life relationships, and experiences that lead him to know that his only hope is peace and love.